BOLDLY ASKING

BOLDLY ASKING

Aletha Hinthorn

Beacon Hill Press of Kansas City
Kansas City, Missouri

Library of Congress Cataloging-in-Publication Data
Hinthorn, Aletha.
    Boldly asking / Aletha Hinthorn.
        p.   cm. — (The satisfied heart series)
    ISBN 0-8341-1605-7
        1. Prayer—Christianity.   2. Spiritual life—Christianity.   I. Title.
II. Series: Hinthorn, Aletha.   Satisfied heart series.
BV215.H56   1996
248.3'2—dc20   95-48370
                                                                  CIP

10   9   8   7   6   5   4

Contents

1

PREPARING YOUR HEART TO COME BOLDLY

*We do God . . . honor by believing what He
has said about Himself and having the cour-
age to come boldly to the throne of grace.*[1]
—*A. W. Tozer*

Introduction

"What helps you pray?" I asked my daughter.

"When I know God loves me, I feel more like praying,"
she replied.

More than anything else, we need to "know and rely on
the love God has for us" (1 John 4:16). According to 1 John 4:8,
"God is love." This verse says more than God loves—it says
His essence *is* love. He cannot help loving us, because He is
made out of love. And because He loves us, He takes great delight in us and rejoices over us with singing (Zeph. 3:17).

God longs for those He loves to enjoy His fellowship.
He enjoys ours! Jesus promises that if we simply open the
door, He "will come in and eat" with us (Rev. 3:20). The
Greek word for *eat* means more than just having a brief snack
together; it means sharing the main meal of the day. He will
do His part to make our fellowship a wonderful celebration.
When we come to worship, He is delighted. As we learn to
come boldly to Him, our greatest delight will be worshiping Him.

7

Discussion and Questions

Jesus encountered the woman at the well—a woman others would not have bothered to speak to. He took time to correct her concept of worship. Why? Because He knew His Father loved her and yearned for her worship.

"God is spirit, and his worshipers must worship in spirit and in truth," Jesus told her (John 4:24). Wanting to encourage her to approach God, He told her that God anticipates the worship of those who come in spirit and in truth. In this study we will consider what kind of God would desire our worship, and what it means to come to Him in spirit and in truth.

◆ Come Expecting a Welcome

1. Probably nothing is more basic to our coming boldly to God than having a correct concept of Him. We're often impoverished because we think of God as a stern or even distant God only slightly interested in us. Which of these faulty statements about God are you sometimes tempted to think?

___ He is an angry judge who watches for our slightest faults.

___ He is a harsh taskmaster who is unhappy if we don't always give Him our best efforts.

___ He is far off and unconcerned with our affairs.

2. God enjoys us and longs for us to welcome His fellowship. We grieve our Heavenly Father far more than we imagine when we act as though we are His servants instead of His friends. What are two of the ways He refers to us in Gal. 4:6-7?

3. Jesus told His disciples, "I have eagerly desired to eat this Passover with you" (Luke 22:15). The Greek is emphatic here. It's as if Jesus said, "I have desired with all my heart to have fellowship with you." How does God describe His joy in us in Isa. 62:5?

God is not looking at us as if He's a reluctant judge showing kindness to a criminal. He loves us with the same intensity with which a groom loves his bride!

4. Think of yourself as God's child. You are not a servant trying to please a master—but a much-loved child whose Father delights in you and rejoices in doing good for you. God is rejoicing over us with all His heart. Read Jer. 32:40-41 and record the phrase that means the most to you.

5. God has recorded what delights Him so we can do what brings Him joy. Look up the following verses and write down what God says pleases Him. Why does knowing these truths help us pray with more confidence?

 Ps. 147:10-11

Note that God is not pleased when we depend upon anything but Him. According to verse 10, what other things might we depend upon?

As you read these verses, consider how you can give God pleasure.

 Prov. 15:8

Luke 12:32

6. The psalmist exclaimed, God "delivered me because He delighted in me" (Ps. 18:19, NKJV). List three evidences of God's love you've seen in the past month. Thank Him for these.

◆ Worship God in Spirit

Jesus told the woman at the well that God is Spirit. Once we understand that God is Spirit, we recognize that our gifts of worship to Him must be of our spirits. Genuine worship does not consist of coming to a certain place or going through a certain ritual. True worship is when our spirit speaks to and meets with God. Through our spirit, we can attain an intimacy with God.

1. We can appear to be worshiping and not be truly worshiping at all. Describe those who do not worship God with their spirits. See Matt. 15:8-9.

2. What are external forms we may adopt that appear to be worship but fail to satisfy God's criteria of worship?

3. Proper worship is, first of all, an inward attitude. Compare the form of worship described in Isa. 29:13 with the worship of our spirits as described in Pss. 4:7; 33:21; 103:1.

4. What are gifts our spirits can give?

We can worship God in spirit—with our mind, desires, heart, our inner being desiring to glorify God—anywhere at any time. God's eyes are seeking those who offer silent gratitude, love, a prayer of concern for others. Try to do this several times through the day today.

A musician who played her flute in the *Messiah* told me what had gone through her mind during performance: "I wonder if the singers are worshiping with those words. Maybe this is just another performance for them." But then she realized she should be thinking differently: "*I* can worship. I'm not very good at saying words of praise, but I'll play my best, and if You can hear my flute in heaven, this is for You, God."

God accepts as worship our best efforts of the moment, when they're offered to Him with love. At first our attempts to draw near Him may simply be acts of our wills—spending our lunch hour with His Word or setting the alarm clock for an earlier morning hour. But even small expressions of love offered to Him are accepted as worship.

The more we're aware of God, the more our spirits long to offer every act, even small ones, as signs that we love Him. "I set this table because I love You," my heart sang one morning as I carefully placed silverware on the table for guests. Every act of housework or every kindness we do for others can be done because we love Him.

5. Read 1 Cor. 10:31. List ways you can consciously worship God with your spirit this week.

When Mary went to see her granddaughters, she took them shopping and offered to buy them each one thing they wanted. The younger girl, as usual, wanted a book. "And what do *you* want?" she asked the other.

"Nothing—I just wanted to be with you," she replied. Sometimes we need to come to God without offering requests but simply desiring to commune with His Spirit.

6. God will lovingly come close as we draw near to Him. Meditate on James 4:8 and write several ways your spirit can honor that invitation.

◆ Worship God in Truth

God seeks those who worship Him "in truth" (John 4:23). To *worship in truth* means we worship without pretension, without hidden motives. We offer worship that expresses a genuine desire to glorify Him.

1. Notice that Ps. 145:18 states that a spirit of truth allows us access into God's presence. Why do you think our coming to God in truth is so important to Him?

2. Read Heb. 4:13. The last phrase in this verse could be translated "we are compelled to meet God's eyes." Everything in our lives comes under the scrutiny of God. Paul says that everything is naked to God, meaning that He sees through all our outward disguises.

William Barclay says the Greek used in Heb. 4:13 was also used in ancient times to describe a situation in which a criminal was being led to execution. A dagger was placed below his chin so he could not bow his head to hide in shame, forcing him to keep his head up so all would see his face.[2] We may avert our gaze from people we are ashamed to meet, but someday we will all meet the eyes of God.

How might our worship change if we thought of worshiping while looking God in the face?

3. The result of worshiping God in truth—being humble and honest so we are unashamed before Him—is "hearts at rest in his presence" (1 John 3:19). What might be some indicators that our hearts are (or are not) at rest in His presence?

4. 1 John 3:19-20 explains that hearts at rest in God's presence have no condemnation. The results are staggering. Read verses 21 and 22 to discover the effectiveness of our prayers when our hearts are at rest in His presence.

5. Also, according to verse 22, what two behaviors indicate that our hearts have no condemnation?

6. Coming to God "in truth" means we are perfectly honest and frank when we talk to Him. He will let us say anything we feel, as long as we say it to Him. What did the psalmist say to God in Ps. 42:9?

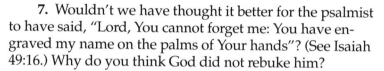

7. Wouldn't we have thought it better for the psalmist to have said, "Lord, You cannot forget me: You have engraved my name on the palms of Your hands"? (See Isaiah 49:16.) Why do you think God did not rebuke him?

8. When we come to God in prayer, we're coming to One who is Light. In His light we see light—we gain understanding. Prayer gives us an opportunity to examine ourselves. What happens if we see a time when we've grieved God, and we don't do anything about it?

 Ps. 66:18

Prov. 28:9

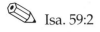 Isa. 59:2

 Isa. 1:15

When Isaiah saw God's glory (Isa. 6:1-8), he knew his precise need. "I am a man of unclean lips," he cried (v. 5). At once God provided the remedy. A live coal from the altar was laid upon his mouth. Only then was Isaiah ready to respond to God's voice.

The Lord knows our exact needs also, and if He reveals anything that is hindering us from worshiping Him in truth, we can ask Him to cleanse us.

Have you claimed His promise in 1 John 1:9?

If you have, "Let us draw near to God with a sincere heart in full assurance of faith" (Heb. 10:22).

Scriptural Role Model

Do you remember the story of Simon, who had a dinner in honor of Jesus? He had plenty of food for all the guests, but he had forgotten the one thing Jesus wanted more than all else. Christ wanted the worship of Simon's spirit, not simply his service.

A woman slipped into their gathering, and as she stood behind Christ she began to weep. She loved Him so much! Her tears fell on His feet, which were behind Him as He reclined at Simon's table. She tenderly wiped them with her hair, kissed them, and poured perfume on them.

None of this was lost on Jesus. He chided Simon for not showing Him love. "You did not give me a kiss, but this woman, from the time I entered, has not stopped kissing my feet" (Luke 7:45).

Jesus is still noticing those who want to communicate their love to Him. He whispers, "I was looking for you," to those who come to worship Him in spirit and in truth (John 4:23).

Memorize

"Search me, O God, and know my heart; test me and know my anxious thoughts. See if there is any offensive way in me, and lead me in the way everlasting" (Ps. 139:23-24).

Prayer

Dear Lord, I long to know and rely on the love You have for me. I want to delight in Your fellowship, to be confident of Your love.

Teach me to worship You with my spirit. May all I do be done out of love for You. I pray this in Jesus' name. Amen.

2
ENTER WITH PRAISE!

Praise, like a straight line, is the shortest distance between a saint and His God![1]
—*Jack Taylor*

Introduction

"How shall I pray now?" The caller was desperate. He had prayed and fasted but could see no evidence that God was answering.

"Why don't you try praise?" I suggested, reminding him that after King Jehoshaphat's army had prayed and fasted, they went forward praising God.

Satan is repelled by praise. The evil spirits controlling the Israelites' enemies became so confused that the enemy soldiers turned upon each other. The Israelites spent three days gathering the spoils from this battle they had won because they expressed their faith in God through praise.

Judges 1 tells that Joshua had just died and the Israelites were faced with fighting their first battle without their leader. They pleaded desperately, "Who will be the first to go up and fight for us against the Canaanites?" (Judg. 1:1).

The Lord replied, "Judah is to go" (Judg. 1:2). The name *Judah* is significant because it means *praise*. Praise is to lead the way when we're approaching the throne of grace.

In this chapter we'll discover that we come into God's holy presence when we praise. We'll consider the power of our praise and, finally, learn how we can practice praise.

Discussion and Questions

Praise turns our focus onto God and His promises.
"God is light; in him there is no darkness at all" (1 John 1:5).
As long as we look at Him, we see no darkness—no dark
nights, no dark clouds, no dark future. It's when we take our
eyes off Him that things look dark.

◆ The Presence of God in Praise

1. Although God is present everywhere, He is actively
present where joyful praise exists. "But thou art holy, O thou
that inhabitest the praises of Israel" (Ps. 22:3, KJV). "Judah
[praise] was his sanctuary [dwelling place]" (Ps. 114:2, KJV).

What is the gate into the presence of God, according to
Ps. 100:4?

2. In Scripture, worship that brought the presence of
God was marked by two things—costliness and extrava-
gance. King Solomon offered 1,000 sacrifices to the Lord.
What was God's response? See 1 Kings 3:4-5.

3. According to 2 Chron. 5:6, the people brought so
many sheep and oxen to be sacrificed that their numbers
"could not be recorded or counted." Two chapters later, their
counted and recorded offerings totaled 22,000 oxen and
120,000 sheep (see 2 Chron. 7:5, KJV). Too many to count
would have been extravagant!

What brought God's presence and glory in 2 Chron.
5:13-14? What was His response to their worship?

4. What costly and extravagant gift can we offer God? In Col. 2:6-7, Paul tells us to "continue to live in" Christ "overflowing with thankfulness." What do you think it means to be *overflowing with thankfulness?* Compare an attitude that is overflowing with thankfulness with one that is overflowing with complaining. Which is a more natural tendency, unless we live in Christ?

5. A costly praise could be one referred to in Heb. 13:15: "Through Jesus, therefore, let us continually offer to God a sacrifice of praise." A sacrifice calls for death; praise often calls for giving up or *slaying* our own opinions of what God should do in our situation. Why would a failure to sacrifice our evaluation of how we want God to respond hinder our giving Him thanks in all circumstances?

Giving thanks can—and should—be done on the basis of God's faithfulness, rather than on our perception of our current situation. How do you think praising God in a difficult situation helps our faith?

When faith takes the tangible form of praise, Satan always flees. Praise casts fiery darts at Satan, and he *cannot* remain in the area. Circumstances may not change, but because praise brings God's presence, our perspective often changes.

Evelyn Christenson, best-selling author of *What Happens When Women Pray*, shivered in her hotel room in Australia

one wintry Sunday evening. Chills from a sore throat, plus
having sat all that day in cold buildings, left her miserable.
She bit into an apple, but her throat hurt too much to swal-
low it. Starting early the next morning, she was scheduled to
speak all day.

   She knelt down by her bed to pray. She didn't ask God
to prepare a replacement speaker, or even to heal her.
Rather she just stayed there, kneeling in prayer, with feelings of gratitude spontaneously flowing to God for the
privilege of once again being absolutely dependent upon
Him. She arose from her knees and was surprised to find
her throat completely healed.[2]

   6. Those who continually praise constantly live in
God's presence. The reverse is also true. When we see God
in His love and power, praise is inevitable—both in heaven
and on earth. When Isaiah and John glimpsed the eternal
world, what did they see happening? Read Isa. 6:1-4 and
Rev. 4:7-11.

   7. Have you experienced, individually or in a group, a
time when praising God either in song, testimony, or
prayer brought God's presence?

◆ The Power of Praise

   "Resist the devil, and he will flee from you" (James 4:7).
Because praise produces the atmosphere in which the divine
presence resides, it is the most effective shield against Satan
and his attacks. In *Destined for the Throne*, Paul Billheimer
suggests that because Satan is allergic to praise, "where there

is massive triumphant praise, Satan is paralyzed, bound, and banished."[3]

1. Praising God brings us into His presence. What does Ps. 16:11 say happens when we are in His presence?

2. What is the benefit of joy, according to Neh. 8:10?

3. Since God dwells in the praises of His people, prayer and praise are devastating to Satan. Read 2 Chron. 20:1-26 for an example of victory through praise. What did God do when the army began to sing and praise? See verse 22.

4. The Bible tells us to praise, more than it tells us to pray. Often we think of praising God after He's answered our prayers; but what do Ps. 40:16 and Phil. 4:6 indicate?

5. Praising allows us to pray with confidence and joy. Consider Col. 1:3-4. Why does praising contribute to Paul's confidence and joy in prayer?

6. By praising God, we take the focus off our problems and put the focus on our loving God, who controls all circumstances. What were some of the difficulties in which the following men chose to give thanks? Consider how their choice to praise God affected them.

a. What did Daniel do when King Darius issued a decree that no one should pray to anyone other than him for 30 days? (See Daniel 6:10.) If you had prayed during such circumstances, would you have been giving thanks? Why do you think Daniel did?

b. What did Paul and Silas do when they were thrown into prison with their feet put in the stocks? (See Acts 16:25.) What might "midnight" signify in your life?

When my mother was in Papua New Guinea, she wrote that one of the missionaries, Miss Ellis, had been sick with fever, headache, and pleurisy. As Miss Ellis lay in bed, Satan whispered, "You're a long way from home."

Jesus immediately whispered, "But you're not very far from Me."

Then the Lord gave her Ps. 50:23: "Whoso offereth praise glorifieth me: and to him that ordereth his conversation aright will I shew the salvation of God" (KJV).

Miss Ellis recalled hearing a paraphrase of that verse: "Who offereth praise glorifieth me, and to him that useth praise over and over again enough to make a trodden road, to him will I show the deliverance of God."

She began "trodding the road of praise." A friend gave her a hot drink and asked if she could do anything. Miss Ellis replied, "Yes, you can help me make a road." A short time later, the Spirit said, "Get up, make your bed, and comb your hair." While doing these things, she was healed.

7. God delights in those who praise Him even when bad things are happening in their lives. Habakkuk said he would rejoice when the fig tree didn't blossom, when the stall was empty—in any desolate circumstance. (See Hab. 3:17-19.) Why? Because God had revealed His power, and Habakkuk saw Him as sovereign. (See verses 1-6.) Habakkuk's praises were based on an increased understanding of God's power, love, and faithfulness. Is it necessary to see God as sovereign to be able to praise Him in all circumstances? Why?

◆ The Practice of Praise

1. "And when you sacrifice a sacrifice of thanksgiving to the Lord, . . . sacrifice it so that you may be accepted" (Lev. 22:29, RSV). Scripture gives at least four conditions of being a thankful worshiper. Match the following scriptures and requirements.

1 Sam. 15:22	A genuine humility
2 Cor. 9:7	Reconciliation with fellow Christians
Luke 18:9-14	A loving and obedient heart
Matt. 5:23-24	A cheerful spirit

To begin practicing the praise of God, let's declare with the psalmist: "My heart is fixed, O God, my heart is fixed: I will sing and give praise" (57:7, KJV). "I will bless the LORD at all times: his praise shall continually be in my mouth" (34:1, KJV). The practice of praise is to be continual, but it will become that only as we discipline ourselves to practice.

Jack Taylor, in *The Hallelujah Factor*, tells of a converted atheist who related how he and his atheist friends would gather in their meetings and take turns publicly blaspheming God. They were so adeptly trained that they could stand for hours and hurl insults and ridicule toward God without ever repeating themselves.[4]

How can we train ourselves to praise God? Perhaps David was so skilled at worship because he did it often. He wrote, "Seven times a day do I praise thee because of thy righteous judgments" (Ps. 119:164, KJV).

One writer commented about Old Testament praise, "Praise was often so exciting that worship could only be described as boisterous. There was dancing (Ps. 150:4), all kinds of instruments (Ps. 108:2), constant singing (Ps. 33:3), and even tumultuous shouting (Ps. 27:6). There was nothing dreary about Old Testament worship! In fact, one has the impression that in praising, men and women have their highest end."[5] How does our worship compare with that described in the Old Testament? Whether or not we express our worship as they did, we should have the same gladness in our hearts.

2. What kinds of sacrifices please God, according to Ps. 69:30-31 and Heb. 13:15-16? Why do you think He wants such gifts?

3. What attributes of God do we need to focus on to "continually offer to God a sacrifice of praise" (Heb. 13:15-16)?

In Ps. 136, God's love is the theme. In each of those 26 verses, one of God's attributes or works is extolled with the refrain "His love endures forever." Jehoshaphat and his army went into battle proclaiming, "Give thanks to the LORD, for his love endures forever" (2 Chron. 20:21). Of all the reasons given in Scripture to praise the Lord, this one could well be the most often repeated! Could it also be the one most easily forgotten?

"I began arising early each morning to spend time worshiping the Lord," reported Ann, a woman hungry for God's presence. "I used the Psalms, singing them to God. After about six months, several people at different times commented, 'Something's different about you.'" Ann's worship brought a fresh sense of God's Spirit into her life.

4. God delights so much in our praise that every word for praise and worship used in the Old Testament teaches something specific about *how* to worship. Use each of these in your own worship:

a. For example, *yadah*, which is used more than 90 times, means "to worship with extended hands, to throw out the hands, to give thanks to God." Read Ps. 107:8 (KJV) and substitute this definition for the word *praise*.

b. Another word, *shabach*, means "to shout, to address in a loud tone." Find this usage in Ps. 63:3.

c. The most frequently used word is *hallel*, which we translate as *hallelujah* or *praise*. The word means "to laud, to boast, to celebrate, to rave." *Hallel* is used repeatedly in Ps. 150. Are we as zealous about praising God as this psalm indicates we should be?

5. God especially delights in our singing praises. At least 41 psalms specifically refer to "singing praises" to the Lord. Since the Hebrew language often emphasized a thought by repeating it, consider the importance to the psalmist of singing, as stated in Ps. 47:6.

a. Why do you think the instruction for combining praise and singing is given so frequently, such as in Pss. 66:1-2; 95:1-2; and 96:1-2?

b. What should we sing during prayer, according to Eph. 5:19 and Col. 3:16?

c. Martin Luther believed the gifts of language and of song were given to humanity so we could proclaim the Word of God through music.[6] Always using someone else's words in our singing, however, may be as undesirable as it would be to always pray someone else's prayers. What kind of song does Ps. 144:9 suggest we sing?

d. What themes do the following verses suggest we use in our singing?

Ps. 59:16

Ps. 69:30

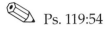 Ps. 119:54

6. Jesus is our model in prayer and praise. For what did He give thanks when He prayed? See John 11:41-44.

The more we rejoice in God's goodness, the more easily we can come with boldness. We can approach a loving God with confidence.

Scriptural Role Model

Worship may be difficult when life is painful and we don't feel like worshiping. Paul and Silas were thrown into prison, but at midnight they began to sing. Perhaps it took them until midnight to get over their discouragement at being prisoners. But once they began praising and singing, God came and accepted their rejoicing and delivered them.

When we deliberately choose to worship, we find God most accepting of our worship. We offer our words, songs, time, effort, and wholehearted participation, and God accepts our offering as abundant, even extravagant.

Memorize

"Do not be anxious about anything, but in everything, by prayer and petition, with thanksgiving, present your requests to God" (Phil. 4:6).

Prayer (adapted from Ps. 103)

Praise the Lord, O my soul; all my inmost being, I praise Your holy name. I praise You as I remember Your benefits—You forgive all my sins and crown me with love and compassion. You satisfy my desires with good things.

Thank You for being compassionate and gracious, slow to anger, abounding in love. Praise the Lord, O my soul.

3

SCRIPTURE-GUIDED PRAYING

Too long have prayer and Bible study been divorced, and with sad results. What God has joined together, we should never have put asunder.[1]   —W. Graham Scroggie

Introduction

"So many of my prayers for my children get in a rut—I pray the same thing day after day," a friend said. "Well, not exactly," she added. "One morning I'll pray, *Do something today, Lord, to make them think about You.* Then the next morning I pray desperately, *Don't let anything happen to them today.* It's almost as though I cancel out yesterday's prayers."

Is there some way we can discern what requests to make? How can we know we're asking God to supply exactly what He sees we need?

God has provided two ways for us to discern what requests we should bring to Him. First, He has given us prayers in Scripture that teach us the kind of requests that please Him. Second, He gives us the Holy Spirit to guide our praying. In this chapter let's consider the impact that praying scripture will have and then discuss ways to turn God's Word into prayer.

Discussion and Questions

Paul encourages us to pray taking "the sword of the Spirit, which is the word of God" (Eph. 6:17). The Old Testament gives examples of such praying. For instance, Daniel spoke to God boldly, because he knew what God had said. He "understood from the Scriptures" that the end of Israel's captivity was drawing near. Then he "prayed to the LORD" (Dan. 9:2, 4).

We can learn much by listening to godly people pray. Let's see what Paul and Jesus considered to be important requests.

◆ How Did Paul and Jesus Pray?

The Holy Spirit anointed Paul to know how to ask for things that would produce spiritual maturity. How could we better use Paul's prayers than to pray them for others, as he did?

1. What are phrases from each of the following passages that you would like to have someone pray for you?

 Eph. 1:17-18

 Eph. 3:16-19

 Phil. 1:9-11

 Col. 1:9

 2 Thess. 1:11

Philem. 6

2. To learn what prayers are good to pray for your minister and others in Christian ministry, consider the requests Paul made for himself. (Remember: We are all involved in ministry; we are all called to fulfill the Great Commission.)

 Rom. 15:30-32

 Eph. 6:19-20

 Col. 4:3-4

 2 Thess. 3:1

3. What are the themes in these prayers of Paul? Write them in your own words.

4. How will others mature spiritually when God answers these petitions?

5. What requests do you commonly pray? How do your requests compare with those Paul prayed?

6. Do our prayers reflect what we genuinely believe to be our most important concerns? What kinds of needs are actually most important? If spiritual concerns are our priority, what is the promise in Matt. 6:33?

7. Prayer for the unsaved should not be neglected. Usually, however, Paul urged believers to pray for other believers, rather than for unbelievers. "Always keep on praying for all the saints" (Eph. 6:18). Why did Paul emphasize praying for other believers? Could it be that as we live as Christ desires, the unsaved will be drawn toward God through our lives? See what Christ promised in John 12:32.

8. If Paul's prayers are answered, how will believers' lives be changed, and how will their interactions with unbelievers be affected?

9. As God answers prayers like those Paul prayed, believers will share their faith, fearlessly proclaim His Word, be filled with the knowledge of His will, and be fruitful in every good work (Philem. 6; Col. 1:9-10; 4:2-4). According to John 13:35, how does God plan to draw unbelievers to himself?

10. Often we think we need to draw others to Christ, but the Holy Spirit does the drawing. If He is lifted up through our lives, others will respond to Christ.

Notice also what Jesus prayed in John 17:9, 20-23. For whom did He pray, and why did He pray for them?

These references to praying for all the saints do not mean we should pray more for the saints than for unbelievers. Rather than being given directions on what to pray for unbelievers, we're given a sense of the depth of desire we should have. We hear from Jesus and Paul their passion—to seek and to save the lost. Jesus prayed with loud cries (Heb. 5:7). Paul said, "Brethren, [with all] my heart's desire and goodwill for (Israel) I long and pray to God that they may be saved" (Rom. 10:1, AMP.).

11. If we consistently prayed as Paul and Jesus did, why would believers be more effective in winning the world?

12. What was the one prayer request Jesus gave His Church? See Matt. 9:37-38.

Again, Jesus' request was not simply that unbelievers would be saved, but that believers would actually get involved in the harvest.

◆ Learning to Pray Scripture

1. J. Oswald Sanders testified how his spiritual life was transformed. "A change came when I learned to use the Scriptures as a prayer book, and to turn what I read, especially in the Psalms, into prayer."[2] Let God use His Word to help you pray more effectively. Notice the power of the Word in the following verses. Consider how these verses apply to prayer.

 Ps. 19:7-9

 Rom. 15:4

2 Tim. 3:16-17

2. To use scripture in prayer, find a verse that speaks the language of your heart, and regularly present it to the Lord. What a boost this is to our faith!

Perhaps our faith is increased because we begin to get God's perspective rather than man's. "In your light we see light" (Ps. 36:9), the psalmist wrote. Apply Ps. 119:130 to prayer.

3. Eavesdrop on some of the most significant prayers ever prayed. You'll notice that men such as David and Daniel were preoccupied with God's character. Read 1 Chron. 29:10-14 and Dan. 2:20-23. Note what they say.

4. What difference does it make in our praying when we, too, remember that God is ultimately the One in control?

5. Many of the psalms were originally written as prayers. When we read them as prayers, we discover that they draw us into God's presence. For instance, turn Ps. 145 into your prayer. What phrases in it especially encourage your faith?

Often prayers in the Psalms help us identify our specific needs when we pray them as if they were our own deepest prayers.

Sue Monk Kidd says that each week she selects a psalm and then daily takes a few moments to pray through it. She tries to live with it throughout the days ahead, returning to it each day, praying it as if it were her own prayer—whispering its pleas for help, or joining in its praise and worship. Slowly the psalm becomes her prayer. Usually by the end of the week she can identify her own personal situation somewhere in it.

She suggests that when it is difficult to identify with the psalmist—for instance, when he writes with vengeance against his enemies—we should think of our "inner" personal enemies such as hatred, deception, greed, fear, pride, lust, and jealousy.

She once found it difficult to pray a section of Ps. 140:10 (RSV): "Let burning coals fall upon them! Let them be cast into pits, no more to rise!" The thought of such vengeance struck her as repulsive, until she realized that she could use it to call down burning coals on one of her *inner* enemies. At the time, she was wrestling with a fear of breast lumps, having had two benign lumps removed. The thought of having to endure another time of waiting and wondering left her weak with fear. Through the psalm she asked God to help her cast fear away, no more to rise. As she entered more deeply into the psalm, she became drawn intimately into God's presence each time she prayed it. Gradually she found the strength to overcome the fear.[3]

6. Our prayers for our children should include promises God has made regarding children. We also can include requests made by other parents in the Bible. To form your own prayer for your children, find verses that give promises to parents, or that indicate His will regarding children. Especially include specific promises the Lord has given you concerning your family. Notice the following scriptures that are prayers parents prayed for their children or promises we can claim for children.

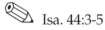 1 Chron. 29:19

 Isa. 44:3-5

 Isa. 49:25

 Ezek. 11:19

(See the sample prayer at the close of this chapter.)

7. As you look for a personal word from God regarding specific needs, the Lord will help you to apply verses others would never have thought of claiming.

For instance, if you're hindered in praying for your grown children because of your personal failures, read Ps. 27:10 and remind God that in the areas you've failed (forsaken) them, He promises to step in. If you're praying about friction in the home or sibling rivalry, what prayer could you pray based on Ps. 147:14? What promise could you claim in Ps. 46:9?

God delights in prayers we pray repeatedly that are based on His Word. Dick Eastman wrote, in *The University of*

the Word, that he had prayed daily a specific prayer for his family based on Luke 2:52. He prayed: "Lord, help my family to grow mentally (in wisdom), physically (in stature), spiritually (with favor toward God), and socially (with favor toward man)." After seven years, God graciously revealed to him precise ways He was answering this prayer.[4]

8. Look at the Lord's Prayer in Matt. 6:9-13 and consider how you could use it in praying for those on your prayer list. (For example, "Give Judy her daily spiritual bread.")

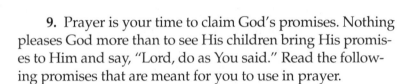

9. Prayer is your time to claim God's promises. Nothing pleases God more than to see His children bring His promises to Him and say, "Lord, do as You said." Read the following promises that are meant for you to use in prayer.

 John 14:14

 John 15:7

 Phil. 4:19

 1 John 5:14-15

Scriptural Role Model

One of Scripture's most instructive prayers is Hannah's prayer of praise in 1 Sam. 2. Several of its points can serve as patterns for our praying.

"My heart rejoices in the LORD" (v. 1), she exclaimed. Often we think of her prayer as a song of thanksgiving for the birth of her son, Samuel. Hannah, however, was worshiping God after she had reared Samuel and presented him to the priest, Eli. The years of daily caring for her son were over. She was soon to go home with empty arms, leaving behind the dear boy who had been the delight of her life.

Only a woman who loved God with all her heart could so rejoice in being able to give her very best to Him. God accepted her worship and gave her more children. Years later, Samuel returned home to Ramah where his parents lived (7:17). What Hannah so willingly gave to God, God gave back to her.

Our magnifying the Lord can begin where Hannah's did. Hannah had a burden; she was barren. We, too, sometimes feel fruitless or helpless in some area of life.

Twice 2 Sam. 1 states that the Lord closed her womb. Hannah believed this. She saw God as the One who gives and the One who takes away. With this knowledge, she could approach God with confidence. Any doubt about whether God was in charge would have destroyed her faith and her ability to glorify Him.

Years after Hannah had prayed for a son, she recalled her time of sorrow and how God had brought deliverance. In this prayer and praise in chapter 2, she did not rejoice because she triumphed over her enemies; she triumphed because she had rejoiced (2:1).

Memorize

"Take the helmet of salvation and the sword of the Spirit, which is the word of God. And pray in the Spirit on all occasions with all kinds of prayers and requests" (Eph. 6:17-18).

Prayer for Children

Dear Father in heaven, I thank You for the gifts of my children. You have lent them to me for a short time, because You love them, and You love me with an everlasting love.

I praise You because You have promised to pour out Your Spirit on my seed and Your blessing on my offspring. Only You know what a blessing from You means in their lives. Only You know how to make them receptive to Your Spirit. Please grant them Your Spirit and Your blessing in Your way.

You have promised to teach my children and to give them peace. Just as You taught David in his youth, teach them and show them Your power. Please grant them spiritual maturity in their youth.

May my children have a heart of flesh—one that is sensitive to, and responsive to, the touch of their God. Give them grace to grow in favor with God and man, just as Jesus did. Give my children the wholehearted devotion to be completely obedient to You, so they may find Your highest plan for their lives.

Give me wisdom to teach them both diligently and tenderly, that they may never become discouraged or sullen. Because Your faithfulness endures to all generations, I praise You for Your perfect provisions for me and my children.

In Jesus' name I pray. Amen.

Scriptures referred to in the prayer above include Isa. 44:3-5; 54:13; Pss. 71:17; 144:12; Luke 2:27; Ezek. 11:19; 1 Chron. 29:19; Deut. 6:7; and Col. 3:21.

4

SPIRIT-GUIDED PRAYING

Prayer is just the breathing of the Spirit in us; power in prayer comes from the power of the Spirit in us, waited on and trusted in.[1]

—*Andrew Murray*

Introduction

"I had a wonderful prayer time today on the way to work," a friend commented recently. Another lady wrote that when she prayed at work, she "felt connected."

Sometimes when we pray we may not feel like praying; we pray simply because we want to be faithful. Then at other times we find it easy to pray—perhaps we sense a great need, or we're aware of how much God loves us. For whatever reason, we feel in touch with God.

Always "pray in the Spirit," Paul instructs in Eph. 6:18. Do we remember it's our privilege to *always* do this? The Holy Spirit within us is "a spirit of grace and supplication" (Zech. 12:10), and we are simply called to beware that we "do not grieve the Holy Spirit of God" (Eph. 4:30).

The Greek word for *Spirit* used in John 14:26 is *paraclete*. To the Greeks, the paraclete was the one who went alongside the man going to trial. In the courtroom, the paraclete was always beside him explaining the issues, helping him see the statements he needed to make, and suggesting actions to take.

Without the Spirit helping us to pray, God would often have to say to us, as Jesus said, "You don't know what you are asking" (Matt. 20:22). Proceeding into prayer without waiting for the Spirit's counsel, we often ask for improper requests, ask with wrong motives, and find it hard to believe.

The study of the fruit of the Spirit will help us be aware of how to prepare our hearts to be sensitive to the Spirit's work in us as we pray.

Discussion and Questions

If we're praying "in the Spirit" or with the help of the Spirit, the attitudes we have when we pray will be the attitudes the Holy Spirit has. The fruit (attitudes) of the Spirit is listed in Gal. 5:22. Can you see how we hinder the Spirit's praying through our spirit if we don't love or if we lack self-control? Let's look at each of the fruits to consider how we can prepare ourselves to pray in the Spirit.

◆ Love

1. If the Spirit helps us pray, we're aware of a strong love. We can ask God to answer our prayers, because He loves those for whom we're praying. Notice that David did this in Ps. 44:3, 26. (Also see 2 Chron. 2:11.)

2. If we truly love someone, we pray as though we're praying for our own need. God wants to love others through us as we pray. How do we receive His love? Read Rom. 5:5.

3. The Holy Spirit is the Spirit of intercession. More often than we realize, the Spirit of intercession within us wants to love those around us through our intercession. But we often don't think of interceding—as we sit in church, while we stand in line at the grocery store, or when we drive. What a great habit it is to lovingly pray for various ones throughout our day! Who could you pray for briefly today?

"You can love more people through prayer than any other way," writes Wesley Duewel. "You can love, by your prayer, people who avoid or resist you. You can love people anywhere in the world by your prayer. The more you pour out God's love through your prayer and actions, the more the Spirit will pour in as you ask Him."[2]

◆ Joy

4. When did Paul pray with joy? Read Phil. 1:4. Do you think his giving thanks (mentioned in v. 3) helped both his faith and his joy? "When you enter His courts with praise, it's like having a direct connection," a friend wrote recently. Paul frequently spoke of giving thanks when he prayed. (See Eph. 1:16 and Col. 1:3.)

5. What does "the joy of the LORD" provide? See Neh. 8:10. Would the joy of the Spirit increase our strength in prayer?

◆ Peace

6. The peace of God is promised to those who do what, according to Phil. 4:6-7?

7. We're not to be anxious about *anything!* (Phil. 4:6). What kinds of things do you tend to be anxious about?

8. How do our anxious thoughts hinder us from being led by the Spirit in our praying?

9. What do the following verses tell us to do to gain peace?

 Isa. 26:3

 1 Pet. 5:7

◆ Patience (Longsuffering, KJV)

10. If we go to prayer with an impatient or unforgiving spirit, the Holy Spirit will not guide our praying. What must we first do, according to Matt. 5:23-24?

11. God "delights in those who . . . hope in His unfailing love" (Ps. 147:11)—especially when we're hoping for His mercy for someone else, perhaps even someone who has wronged us. Read this scripture.

12. Are our prayers Spirit-led if we are impatient with the one for whom we intercede? What words or attitudes in our prayers might help us identify a lack of divine patience in our hearts?

◆ Kindness (Gentleness, KJV)

Kindness is the opposite of severity. If in our praying we keep in step with the Spirit, we have sympathy with those who have failed. Instead of focusing on faults, we focus on loving.

One man told of beginning to pray for a fellow pastor by saying, "O God, You know that brother—" Immediately the Holy Spirit stopped him and rebuked him for judging. His role was not to accuse his Christian brother. Satan is the accuser (Rev. 12:10). While confessing his sin of judging, he remembered this verse: "If there be any praise, think on these things" (Phil. 4:8, KJV). He began to praise God for the man's hard work, his tact, his faithfulness. Later, he learned that while he had been praising, God gave his friend a spiritual uplift.

13. The Spirit leads us to pray for the person from God's perspective. He loves the individual with an everlasting love. If our prayers are filled with negative criticism, we needn't expect them to be answered. Such praying is not Spirit-led. We grieve the Holy Spirit when we're unkind. Read Eph. 4:30-32.

14. If we think others unworthy of our kindness, do you think our attitude is interpreted by God as contempt for His kindness? See Rom. 2:4.

Sometimes we're tempted to think that harshness will bring people to our way of thinking. But God knows that kindness is much more effective. When we think with kindness toward those we pray for, we prepare our hearts for the Spirit to pray through us.

◆ Goodness

If we possess the fruit of goodness, we will be guileless—without hypocrisy. Such praying is solely for God's glory rather than for personal benefit.

15. Wrong motives, bitterness, or subtle desire for praise often come to light when the Spirit is guiding our praying. What would be some questions we could ask ourselves to discern the motives behind our requests?

16. If we pray in the Spirit, what danger mentioned in James 4:3 will we avoid?

If we pray for carnal desires, the Spirit becomes quiet within us. We discover we are praying on our own. It's as though the Holy Spirit is saying, "I can't approve that prayer. You may mean well, but you are not asking for My desires." As we listen to the Spirit, He will guide us to a better way of praying.

Evelyn Christenson wrote,

While our Kurt was taking his entrance exams for a doctoral program in physics, I spent the three hours in prayer. Not knowing how to pray for three whole hours on the same subject, I asked God to teach me. One of the amazing things He showed me was that, although I sincerely was praying for God's will, some of my motives for wanting Kurt to pass those tests were wrong. It was God waving His yellow caution flag, "Watch it!"

Creeping into what I thought were only pure motives about God's will for my son's future was a wrong motive—pride. I found myself praying a seemingly normal, motherly prayer: "Oh, God what if Kurt's cousin Paul passes his tests and gets into his biomedical engineering program and our son flunks?" God's rebuke set me praying for forgiveness for the wrong motive in my praying. God delights in and hears the prayers of those who don't care who gets the glory and the credit. Every prayer which is prayed "in the Spirit" must be prayed because we want God to receive glory.[3]

List several examples of questions we should ask to determine if our prayers are for our glory or for His. For example, "Do I want my friend to be saved so I'll be thought of as a soul winner?"

17. Think of a prayer you want answered. What would be proper and improper motives for this request?

◆ Faithfulness (Faith, KJV)

18. We pray Spirit-led prayers when we pray knowing God hears and will answer. Since Paul tells us to pray always in the Spirit (Eph. 6:18), we should always pray with confidence He will answer. What does Heb. 11:5-6 tell us about how God views faith?

Satan wants us to think we're unable or unworthy to trust. He wants us to forget that God is delighted when we come believing His promises. As we pray in the Spirit more, we find it easier simply to take God at His Word.

Hannah Whitall Smith said she had a friend whose Christian life was a life of bondage. She worked for her salvation as though she were a slave. For instance, she never felt as if the day could go right for her or her family unless she started it with a long season of agonizing prayer—"winding up her machine," Hannah called it.

One day her friend wondered what Christ meant when He said His yoke was easy and His burden light. Hannah asked her, "What would you think of children that had to agonize with their parents every morning for their necessary food and clothing?"

"Of course that would be all wrong," her friend said, adding, "but then, why do I have such good times after I have gone through these conflicts?"

This puzzled Hannah for a moment, but then she asked, "What brings about those good times finally?

"Why, finally," the friend replied, "I come to the point of trusting the Lord."

"Suppose you should come to that point to begin with?" Hannah asked.

"Oh," she replied, with new understanding, "I never until this minute thought that I might!"[4]

To build your faith, learn to rest in God's promises. Ask God to give a special promise on which you can rely for your need. Hold the promise before God in prayer as you plead that scripture again and again.

If God has helped you believe a promise in the past, that promise is still good. Continue believing what the Spirit has enabled you to believe in the past. His Word endures forever.

◆ Gentleness (Meekness, KJV)

The Greek word for *gentleness* means humility. If we want to be in harmony with the Holy Spirit, we must have a teachable spirit. "Receive with meekness the engrafted word, which is able to save your souls" (James 1:21, KJV).

19. Often the Holy Spirit wants to teach us through the Word how to pray or how not to pray. Do you recall a time when the Spirit taught you that your request was not scriptural, or a time when He taught you how to refocus your praying?

Carole and Jack Mayhall offered counsel in a heartbreaking situation in which a pastor friend had left his wife for his secretary. Soon after the counseling session, Carole and Jack went on their annual two-week time in the mountains for study, prayer, and writing.

During their first morning in the mountains, Carole's heart felt heavy. Why was she depressed? she wondered. She had so looked forward to this getaway. When she did a little digging, she realized she was still preoccupied with their friends' situation. The Lord reminded her, "Whatever is true, whatever is noble, whatever is right, whatever is pure, whatever is lovely, whatever is admirable—if anything is excellent or praiseworthy—think about such things" (Phil. 4:8).

The Lord questioned her heart: "Carole, what you are thinking about—is it true, admirable . . . ?" The Lord took her through the whole list, and she realized her thoughts met only one of the eight qualifications on His list.

The Lord wanted to teach her to focus on Him. Because she meekly accepted the teaching of the Holy Spirit, her prayers were not hindered.[5]

20. There is a "humility that comes from wisdom" (see James 3:13). What are the marks of our wisdom if it is from the Holy Spirit? See verse 17.

◆ Self-control (Temperance, KJV)

21. Children learn that self-control is "doing something even when I don't feel like it." It is sometimes defined as "instant obedience to the initial promptings of the Holy Spirit." How would these definitions of self-control relate to praying in the Spirit?

A lady in New Zealand lived in a little village where there was no teaching about the Holy Spirit, but she had heard someone mention praying in the Spirit.

Hungering for the Spirit, she prayed, "'God, I've heard that people can pray with a spirit of prayer—so, Lord, give me Your Spirit of prayer.'" God filled her with His Spirit and, in response to her specific request, gave her a burden for five young men. She faithfully prayed for these young men, and they are now all men of God.

22. Do you want the Spirit to help you pray? Claim His promise in Luke 11:13.

Scriptural Role Model

Paul's written prayers were certainly prayed in the Spirit. See if you can find at least six of the fruit of the Spirit in the following verses.

I thank my God every time I remember you. In all my prayers for all of you, I always pray with joy because of your partnership in the gospel from the first day until now, being confident of this, that he who began a good work in you will carry it on to completion until the day of Christ Jesus.

It is right for me to feel this way about all of you, since I have you in my heart; for whether I am in chains or defending and confirming the gospel, all of you share in God's grace with me. God can testify how I long for all of you with the affection of Christ Jesus.

And this is my prayer: that your love may abound more and more in knowledge and depth of insight, so that you may be able to discern what is best and may be pure and blameless until the day of Christ, filled with the fruit of righteousness that comes through Jesus Christ—to the glory and praise of God *(Phil. 1:3-11)*.

Memorize

"And pray in the Spirit on all occasions with all kinds of prayers and requests" (Eph. 6:18).

Prayer

Holy Spirit, teach me to pray. Deeply possess me and enable me to pray the prayers You long to answer. Touch my desires, my faith, and my ability to persevere. Provide all I need to pray always in the Spirit. I ask this in the powerful name of Jesus. Amen.

5

WHAT DO I DESIRE?

Perfect prayer is not attained by the use
of many words, but through deep desire.[1]
—Catherine of Siena

Introduction

"We really don't deeply desire very many things, do we?"
a friend sighed, as we thought on Mark 11:24—"What
things soever ye desire, when ye pray, believe that ye receive them, and ye shall have them" (KJV).

Nothing is more important in prayer than to hunger
for what the Spirit wants to give. One afternoon I was
praying for a missionary nurse in Papua New Guinea.
"Help her win someone to You today in the clinic" seemed
to be a Spirit-implanted desire. The Spirit helped me pray
until I was confident God had heard. About 10 days later,
the length of time it takes to receive a letter from there, a
letter from the nurse arrived, saying, "Today two men
came to the Lord in the clinic!"

A Spirit-implanted desire will often differ from our
natural desires. We can test our desires by asking, "Am I
longing for God? Is He the end of my quest? Will all my
desire be satisfied if I have more of Him in my situation?"
The deepest passion of Jesus was to bring glory to God.
Our desires must reflect His.

When we can say with all of our heart, "More of God
will completely satisfy me," then we are ready for the Holy
Spirit to express His longings through us. We find ourselves

saying with Phillip, "Lord, show us the Father—cause us to see the Father, that is all we ask; then we shall be satisfied" (John 14:8, AMP.).

When the Holy Spirit implants a desire within us in prayer, we can pray with faith, because God never gives us a desire to pray for anything that He does not plan to answer. "This is the confidence we have in approaching God: that if we ask anything according to his will, he hears us. And if we know that he hears us—whatever we ask—we know that we have what we asked of him" (1 John 5:14-15).

Discussion and Questions

"But you, dear friends . . . pray in the Holy Spirit" (Jude 20). Our goal in prayer is to learn what the Holy Spirit desires to do and then to let Him express that longing through us.

The following questions can help us recognize and follow the desires of the Spirit. How would you respond to each of these questions?

◆ What Do I Desire?

1. *Do I respond when the Spirit gives me a desire or an inclination to pray?*

a. If we are willing to intercede, God will make us aware of others' needs. The nudge to pray may simply be an awareness that Susan is discouraged or that Kent is withdrawing from church. Developing a sensitivity to the thoughts God places in our minds can help our praying be Spirit-directed. What do the following two verses say about God's desire to communicate needs to us?

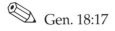 Gen. 18:17

 Amos 3:7

b. What an honor it is when the Spirit gives us a hunger to pray for someone! Have you ever felt drawn to pray for someone and later learned that person was in need?

2. *Do I expect the Spirit to teach me what to pray?*

a. We would often agree with Paul when he said, "We do not know what we ought to pray for" (Rom. 8:26).

"Delight yourself in the Lord and he will give you the desires of your heart" (Ps. 37:4). We often understand this verse to mean that as we delight ourselves in Him, God will grant our desires. That is certainly one of the applications. However, it also could be teaching us that as we delight ourselves in Him, He will give us the desires He wants us to have.

Have you ever begun praying and found your request changing because a different request seemed to be more pleasing to the Holy Spirit?

b. If God's presence is gently leading, we know that to pray in a certain way would please God. To pray in the Spirit is to follow this quiet leading. A need may be impressed upon our hearts, and we find we can offer this need to God with strong desire. How does Acts 15:28 teach that it's possible to be aware of what the Holy Spirit approves?

Kenneth Taylor paraphrases Eph. 6:18, "Ask God for anything in line with the Holy Spirit's wishes" (TLB). When you have a listening spirit, God will direct you to pray correctly. When you don't know what to pray, be quiet before God, and be sensitive to what desires the Spirit will enable you to pray.

c. What is the promise of John 14:26? How can we apply this to our praying?

3. *When God's Spirit guides me to a specific desire, do I pray until it is given?* The strength of our desires will be tested. God delights in those who are determined to have His answer. In Luke 11:5-8, what was necessary for the man to do to receive bread from his neighbor?

The Holy Spirit scrutinizes our desire, our perseverance, and responds to what is in us. Receiving the desire to pray from the Spirit—even for a personal need—is an infinite honor. We should cling to such an honor. "Ask and keep on asking, and it shall be given you" (Luke 11:9, AMP.).

4. *Do I indicate small desires to God by spasmodic praying?*
Often we sense a desire, pray once, and then forget the need.
But God gives the rest and confidence of faith to the faithful.
Let's be "followers of them who through faith and patience
inherit the promises" (Heb. 6:12, KJV). Why do you think
faithfulness often deepens our desires?

5. *When the Spirit gives me a desire to pray for someone else,
do I pray as though I am interceding for a personal need?* We pray
best for those we love most. Matt. 15:22-28 tells of a Canaan-
ite woman who came to Jesus begging Him to heal her
daughter. What was her prayer in verse 25? Why do you
think she stated her request as she did?

6. *Do I seek to feel the depth of yearning the Spirit feels?*
Read Rom. 8:26. It is Christlike for us to be so filled with
compassion that at times we pray with tears. Although it
would be hypocritical to seek tears, we should welcome the
tears when the Holy Spirit gives them. Consider some of the
many references to those who wept in prayer. What do you
think their tears indicated?

 Job 30:25

 Jer. 13:17

 2 Cor. 2:4

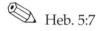 Heb. 5:7

"Desire is another word for hunger. Unless there is sighing, longing, hungering and thirsting, and perhaps even tears of desire, you have probably not yet reached prevailing prayer."[2]

7. *Do I express my desires to God by keeping a prayerful attitude throughout my day?*

a. In Exod. 30:34-38, God described our prayer as incense to be offered to Him. A portion of the incense was to be beaten very small and kept constantly ready to light (v. 36). This teaches us that we are continually to maintain a prayerful attitude. Our incense cannot always be rising in cloud after cloud to heaven. God accepts and values a prayerful spirit within us, ready to be kindled at all times.

Unless we have distinct times of prayer, however, we won't have the aroma of devotion diffused throughout our day. Twice a day, morning and evening, the priest came with his pan of coals and incense. During the intervening hours between these two sacrifices, there was a faint but continual fragrance.

We should not lump our worship into one part of our day and leave the rest of our day without it. There must be the smoldering all day long. According to 1 Thess. 5:16-19, what attitudes should continually be in our hearts?

b. It's easier to pray with strong desires if we've lifted our requests to God continually throughout the day. Satan fights our keeping the incense of our desire burning before the Lord. Why is continually lifting our needs to God important in showing Him we are sincere?

c. To have fervent desires when we pray, it will help if we keep bringing our minds back to God. Those who seek Him with all their hearts find Him. And if our seeking Him includes looking for Him in the ordinary routine of our everyday lives, we'll find Him there. Apply the promise of Matt. 5:6 to our need to maintain a prayerful attitude.

8. *Do I pray words or clichés almost without thinking?*

Prayers prayed without strong desire can fall under the warning of Eccles. 5:1-2: "Go near to listen. . . . Do not be quick with your mouth, do not be hasty in your heart to utter anything before God. God is in heaven and you are on earth, so let your words be few."

"Weigh thy words, feel deeply, think much, speak little. . . . Send up the silent breathings of your soul," commented Adam Clarke on this passage.

Words spoken with little thought, clichés repeated until we don't think about their meaning—these can become vain repetition. We're not to offer up to God words that cost us no thought. What phrases or forms of prayer do you habitually use?

9. *Do I indicate my desires for Him in small ways?*

a. Strong desire begins with a tiny desire—but how easy it is to quench small desires simply by ignoring the Spirit's drawing! We welcome the Spirit through small actions. What are some ways you can show God your desires are for Him?

b. God, who reads the thoughts and attitudes of our hearts, notices the tiny things we do to show Him our desire for Him. What minor—but significant—action in Luke 19:2-6 indicated to Jesus that He would be welcomed gladly?

One night I stayed up to pray but soon went to sleep on my knees. I awoke and thought of going to bed but decided, "No, I'll try to pray again." Again I went to sleep. The next morning as the Lord was near, helping me to pray, He seemed to say, "I saw your effort to pray and am rewarding you for it." God notices our efforts to draw near to Him, even when we've felt they might have been a waste of time or simply a routine. He sees them and interprets them as desire.

10. *Is prayer as important to me as it is to Jesus?*

When we begin to let the Holy Spirit express His desires through us, we find prayer becoming the most significant part of our lives. Sometimes we express our desires by saying we were born to shop, or we live to play golf. What does Jesus live to do? See Heb. 7:25. How can we indicate to God that our purpose in life reflects Jesus' purpose?

Scriptural Role Model

The barren Shunammite women received the joy of her life—a little boy given by God—because of her kind hospitality to Elisha. She delighted in this little fellow. We can only imagine the depth of her grief the day he became ill and died.

She set out to do all in her power to restore this child. She felt she must reach the man of God. Would her husband share her faith that their son could be restored? Perhaps she knew he wouldn't, so she didn't share her grief with him. She couldn't afford to discuss the risks of this journey she knew she must make to the man of God.

Elisha saw that her distress was so great that she could barely speak of it. She mentions it only indirectly: "Did I desire a son of my lord? did I not say, Do not deceive me?" (2 Kings 4:28, KJV). It was as if she said, "Wasn't the idea of a son your promise? Because you promised me a son, I know you will keep your promise." Elisha understood her unspoken words and commanded his servant, "Go take my staff and lay it on the child."

The Shunammite woman didn't accept that answer. Sending the servant wasn't enough. Someone besides Elisha helping would not satisfy her desire for God's intervention. She showed her desire by saying, "As surely as the LORD lives and as you live, I will not leave you" (2 Kings 4:30). So Elisha followed her.

Her day of agony ended with joy because she followed her heart's deep, God-given desire.

Memorize
"He fulfills the desires of those who fear him; he hears their cry and saves them" (Ps. 145:19).

Prayer
O Lord Jesus, give me the desires You want me to have. Alert me when my prayers are motivated more by self-interest than by desire for God's glory. May my human desires and Your desires merge. Then teach me not to be distracted but to cherish those longings and to follow through with consistent, earnest prayer. In joyous anticipation I pray. Amen.

6

PRAYER LISTS—PRAYER OR RECITATION?

*Let your prayer-list bear the names of those
for whom you pray. . . . Thus the Inner
Chamber will really become a wonder of
God's goodness and a fountain of great joy. It
will become the most blessed place on earth.*[1]
                     —Andrew Murray

Introduction

Does following a prayer list each day have merit? If I can't spend extended time praying for all those on my list, do I accomplish anything by bringing their names before the Lord?

These questions had occurred to me before I heard Jack Hayford tell the following story on *Focus on the Family* on the 1992 National Day of Prayer. One morning after Dr. Hayford's father read devotions at breakfast, he noted to his wife that Exod. 28 tells the priests to bear the names of the 12 tribes on their shoulders to the Lord. When they went to stand before the Lord, it would be a memorial to God.

Mr. Hayford suggested that they bring their families' names, Hayford and Farnsworth, to the Lord each morning and simply say, "Lord, today we hold before You everyone anywhere living named Hayford, and everyone anywhere living named Farnsworth. We pray that You would let Your blessing be upon them, and that there would be some opportunity for any of these to whom we are related by blood to come to know Your Son. In Jesus' name, Amen." Praying this prayer became their daily pattern.

About seven or eight months later, a man called and asked, "Is this Jack Hayford?" Mr. Hayford Sr. replied that it was.

The man said, "I'm in town on a business trip, and my last name is also Hayford. Lately I've started looking in phone books wherever I am to see if there are any other Hayfords." They asked about each others' families, and when Mr. Hayford Sr. mentioned he had two sons in the ministry, the man shared that he was a Christian. "You know," the man said, "it's exciting to get to share that with you and to find another Hayford that's a Christian. I received the Lord only about five months ago."

After the Hayfords started to pray for those named Hayford and Farnsworth, on three occasions—through unusual encounters of people seeking them out—they learned of people named Hayford who had come to Christ during that year. The Hayfords said they believed God gave them those encounters to confirm that their prayers were being heard and that this was a very valid principle.

When we commit ourselves to bringing names to the Lord daily, our prayers are powerful. Such praying is not just a recitation. It provides the Holy Spirit with access to those hearts.

Discussion and Questions

Sometimes we may feel we are shortchanging a need by simply mentioning it briefly in prayer. Fortunately, God gives a firm scriptural foundation for this method of praying.

Peter instructs, "Prepare your minds for action" (1 Pet. 1:13). Having a prayer list is one way to come to God with a prepared mind.

◆ Prayer Lists in Scripture

1. Although we can't develop a prayer life mechanically, all who leave prayer to the impulse of the moment neglect the power of systematic intercession. Five specific times the apostle Paul spoke of mentioning or remembering his fellow Christians in prayer:

Rom. 1:9-10

Eph. 1:16

1 Thess. 1:2

Philem. 4

2 Tim. 1:3

2. What words indicate that Paul prayed for others regularly?

 Rom. 1:8-9

 Eph. 1:16-17

 1 Thess. 1:2

 2 Tim. 1:3

3. Repetition in prayer is scriptural. How many times did Elijah plead with God? See 1 Kings 18:42-45.

We are to ask and keep on asking. Elijah prayed seven times, the number of perfection. In Gen. 18:16-33, Abraham stopped at six times, the number that represents our human frailty.

J. Edwin Orr recalls that when he was 17 he met a missionary who promised to pray for him daily. Occasionally the missionary wrote to him. At the end of World War II, Orr found the missionary dying in the Mildmay Hospital in London. After sharing news and views, Orr asked him lightly, "Did you keep your word to pray for me each day?"

A shadow came across the missionary's face. "No, I'm sorry I can't say that." Then he brightened. "However, I don't think I missed you more than twice, but the pain was very bad those days." Orr said he went away ashamed, yet humbly grateful. The missionary's name was Ernest Hudson Taylor.[2]

◆ Feel Responsible

1. God asks two things of us when we bring a list of names to Him. We see this in Exod. 28 where Aaron, as the representative of the children of Israel, was told to bear the names of the 12 tribes before the Lord. We are to be Aarons, the priests, in the New Testament Church. See 1 Pet. 2:5, 9 and Rev. 1:6.

2. Aaron was to bear the names of the children of Israel two places—his shoulders and his heart. First, let's consider the significance of bearing names on our shoulders. See Exod. 28:12.

The shoulders represent the place for carrying burdens. This indicated that Aaron was to feel responsible for the 12 tribes. God is still looking for those who are willing to assume a sense of responsibility for others.

3. When Queen Esther heard of the threat to her people, she could have said, "*My* life isn't on the line. I'm safe here in the palace, so I'm not going to get involved." But what were her words? See Esther 8:6.

Esther couldn't bear to think of her people perishing. God delights to hear the prayers of those who say, "I can't stand the thought of that person failing spiritually. I'll do what I can to prevent it."

4. Read Exod. 17:8-16. Who does verse 13 say won the battle?

5. Who do you think would have been responsible if the battle had been lost?

6. Sometimes when others stumble spiritually, could it be that we bear some of the responsibility because we failed to pray for them as the Spirit wanted?

How serious is it when we fail to pray for others, according to 1 Sam. 12:23? To whom should you be able to say Samuel's words?

In *Common Sense Christian Living*, Edith Schaeffer recalls being a girl in Shanghai, skipping beside Dr. Hoste, the director of the China Inland Mission. He didn't turn her away but simply told her he was praying and that she could come along if she wished.

She walked with him a number of times, holding his hand and being very quiet while he prayed. She wrote, "He prayed for each missionary in the China Inland Mission, and for each of their children by name. He had the list with him, and he went through it. It was not just a recitation of names; he cared about each person and knew something of their needs. He felt this was his work."[3]

7. The total responsibility, however, does not rest with those praying. If those for whom we're praying are fighting the battle, as the Israelites were in Exod. 17:8-16, and if there is sufficient prayer, victory is inevitable. But Samuel encouraged the people for whom he prayed to do their part. What would happen if they didn't? See 1 Sam. 12:24-25.

8. Paul commended Epaphras to the Colossians by saying he was working hard for them. What was Epaphras doing, according to Col. 4:12?

9. Do you think this meant he felt responsible to God for them? Will we regularly pray or be "always wrestling in prayer" for anyone for whom we don't feel responsible?

10. We show God we've assumed responsibility for others' spiritual needs by regularly bringing their needs to Him. Sometimes we act as though God's faithfulness to answer our prayers depends upon how we feel, instead of remembering that His dependability to hear and answer rely

upon His promises, not our feelings. "I don't feel like praying, so what's the use?" we're tempted to think. What do the following verses say about God's reliability?

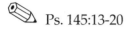 Ps. 145:13-20

 Titus 1:2

◆ Love Them

1. Second, Aaron was to wear the names of the 12 tribes on the breastplate that was over his heart. See Exod. 28:29.

2. The heart represents the seat of our affections and symbolizes the love and personal interest the Lord requires us to have for the people for whom we intercede.

In Phil. 1:7 Paul said he was confident God heard his prayers for them because Paul could say, "I have you in my heart." What do you think it means to have someone in your heart?

3. After having open-heart surgery, our pastor often told the congregation that if the doctor had looked, he would have seen our names on his heart. We sensed his love and his commitment to help us spiritually. Whose names are on your heart? Whose names can the Lord count on us bringing into His presence?

4. One church leader, who travels by car a great deal in his work, prays for the pastors and their families as he drives. He commented that the roster of ministers for whom he is responsible in his denomination takes him about 200 miles. Do you have traveling time to use for prayer?

5. My cousin carries a prayer list in his pocket. When he has some waiting time, he looks at the list and prays for those listed on it. That habit must please God, since He, too, keeps our names before himself. Where does He keep our names, according to Isa. 49:16?

Who should we bring before the Lord regularly? Jesus is not willing that any should perish. (See 2 Pet. 3:9.) Are there those for whom He has given you a desire to pray because you too are not willing for them to fail to make it to heaven? Then put their names on your prayer list. Take time to think where prayer is needed and what concerns draw your heart most.

6. When we pray regularly for the same people, we begin to focus the mighty weapon of prayer on specific individuals. For whom does 1 Tim. 2:2 suggest we pray regularly?

7. What suggestions can the following verses give us for our prayer list?

Ps. 2:8

(Could this be a suggestion to have at least one country on our prayer list?)

Matt. 5:44

(Would anyone in your life qualify?)

8. Who did Samuel feel responsible to pray for regularly? See 1 Sam. 12:19-23.

(Would this imply that we should include those who are under our leadership either at work or at home?)

Daily bringing someone's name before the Lord has powerful results. Dick Eastman tells of a Sunday School teacher who helped bring many students to Christ. After her death, her diary was found to contain such resolutions as "Resolved to pray for each scholar by name. Resolved to wrestle in prayer for each scholar by name. Resolved to wrestle for each by name and expect an answer."[4]

Our feeling of responsibility and love will deepen as we pray. God doesn't entrust with a prayer burden those who scarcely pray, but if we regularly come to Him with specific requests, He'll see us as ones He can bless with a deepening concern for those we love.

Scriptural Role Model

Surely Paul did not spend his entire prayer time praying for every specific need of each Christian. Instead, he confidently lifted them before God, fully trusting God to bless each of them.

Paul said he prayed with confidence. He knew that no prayer was ever lost. Whether or not he could discern God's activity in a person's life, he was sure God was working.

We can learn phrases to pray from Paul's short prayers. He often closed his epistles with short benedictions. For instance, he ends his second epistle to Timothy with "The Lord be with your spirit" (2 Tim. 4:22).

Isn't that a prayer we often would have time to pray for a whole list of people?

Memorize

"As for me, far be it from me that I should sin against the LORD by failing to pray for you. And I will teach you the way that is good and right" (1 Sam. 12:23).

Prayer

Dear Father, will I someday say, "But Lord, if I had known You were going to answer all those prayers, I would have prayed more; I would have put more people on my list"? By that time I will have said farewell to the "sweet hour of prayer." How thankful I am that I still have time to touch others with my love and prayer. Guide me to pray for all those You want to love through me. Thank You for hearing me. Amen.

7

TEACH ME, LORD, TO WAIT

*I think Christians fail so often to get answers
to their prayers because they do not wait
long enough on God. They just drop down
and say a few words, and then jump up and
forget it and expect God to answer them.
Such praying always reminds me of the
small boy ringing his neighbor's door-bell,
and then running away as fast as he can go.*[1]
—E. M. Bounds

Introduction

In her book *When the Heart Waits,* Sue Monk Kidd maintains
that we're a nation of quickaholics.[2] We have fast-food
restaurants, jiffy markets, instant coffee, express lanes, and
express mail. We can get our eyeglasses in an hour, and our
engine oil changed in 10 minutes. Fast-food restaurants were
timed recently in Pittsburgh, and the winner took 45 seconds
to serve a hamburger, fries, and a soft drink. The loser? A
"slow" 3 minutes.

The danger is that the lure of the quick and easy will
seep into our relationship with God. Jesus said for the disciples to go into Jerusalem to wait—to wait for the promise of
the Father. In Luke they were told to tarry until they received
power. Expectant waiting still yields fulfilled promises and
power.

Discussion and Questions

Waiting involves more than time. The word *wait* in the Old Testament corresponds well to the New Testament word *watch*—as when Jesus asked His disciples to watch with Him one hour. They were to do more than simply sit there waiting for time to pass.

The Hebrew word *wait* actually means *twisted,* as a cord is twisted, or as Adam Clarke explains, *wait* means the extension of a cord from one point to another.[3] This is a great metaphor! God is one point, our heart is the other, and the extended cord between both is our intense desire. Waiting is going before the Lord with an earnest desire and looking to Him until He fulfills our desire.

After considering what God meant when He asked us to wait, we'll look at the tremendous benefits of waiting, how to wait, and finally how to know we're waiting.

◆ What Is Waiting?

1. Our strong desire is demonstrated by a listening ear, a heart responsive to God, and faith that God will answer. Which of these are described in the following verses?

 Ps. 62:5

 Ps. 33:20

 Prov. 20:22

2. The expression "Wait for the Lord" implies we're willing to operate on God's time rather than our own. We may cry, "How long, O Lord?" but we still hold onto confident assurance. See Ps. 27:13-14.

3. God always rewards our active, energetic waiting if it's accompanied with obedience. See Ps. 37:34. Why would waiting be incomplete without our obedience? Why does disobedience show God our waiting is insincere?

◆ Why Wait?

1. God gives more promises to those who wait than to any others except those who have faith. (Waiting is actually a *form* of faith, however.) What are some of the rewards of waiting on the Lord, according to the following verses? (Note that the NIV sometimes translates *wait* as *hope*.)

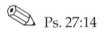 Ps. 27:14

 Ps. 25:3

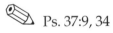 Ps. 37:9, 34

 Isa. 40:31

2. The highest honor we can give God is to wait on Him in simple faith. Compare Isa. 64:4 with 1 Cor. 2:9. Note the word change, which tells us how we can show God we love Him.

3. Do you think it's equally true that *not* waiting indicates a lack of love for God? Why?

4. Although *wait* means *submit* or *supplicate*, it also involves time. Notice the disciples' declaration to wait on God—not on tables—in Acts 6:4. What difference do you think this deliberate choice made in their ministry?

5. We're spiritually emaciated if we don't wait. Why do hurried attempts to pursue spiritual growth result in shallow spiritual progress?

It is essential that we learn to wait for God during our prayer time. Our real determination to wait and to trust God will appear first in our praying.

◆ How Do We Wait?

1. *Choose to wait.* Waiting involves planning to wait, a deliberate choosing to wait on God. The five wise virgins came prepared with extra lamp oil to wait through the night—but not the foolish virgins. They brought only the oil that was in their lamps, because they didn't expect to wait. Often we don't prepare to wait, so we miss the transcendent. "We will wait upon thee," determined Jeremiah (14:22, KJV).

What choices might show God that you are waiting on Him?

2. *Don't look at circumstances.* Our ability to wait doesn't depend upon surroundings or appearances. It hinges simply on our choice to hope when there appears to be no hope.

a. Jesus gave a parable to teach His disciples that they should always pray and not give up. See Luke 18:1-8. Why do you think the widow kept coming despite no apparent hope?

b. Verse 7 reveals that at times God delays our answer. What encouragement should we take from this verse if we think our prayers will never be answered?

c. The secret is in our learning to wait—for "they that wait upon the LORD shall . . . not faint" (Isa. 40:31, KJV). What does Mic. 7:7 promise to those who wait?

If we are patiently waiting, we don't tolerate distractions. Keeping the cord of desire extended from our hearts to God is not easy. We're easily distracted, even when God's answer is our strong desire.

Recently I was seeking the Lord's help for some work I had to do. The Holy Spirit was helping me pray when the doorbell rang. I started for the door but then heard the UPS truck leave and knew the driver had left a package outside my door.

At that moment I had a choice. I could have shown the Lord I was truly waiting on Him. But, I thought, I'll just bring the package in and then continue praying.

I was surprised to see that the package was a dress I had ordered. I almost succeeded in putting it aside. But no, I thought—it wouldn't hurt just to take a peak at it. By the time I had looked at the dress and decided it was too large, the spirit of prayer had gone. The hunger to know God's answer, to hear Him speak, had been deferred by a minor interruption. It was almost as if the Spirit, who is very sensitive to our desires, read from my actions, "She doesn't want Me as much as she said." I realized I had lost an opportunity to demonstrate to the Holy Spirit how very much I wanted His presence.

3. *Be aware of our dependency.* Perhaps the biggest help in learning to wait is a consciousness that we can't make it without the Spirit's help.

a. Notice in the following verses the phrases that indicate our inability to do anything in our own strength.

 1 Chron. 29:14

 1 Cor. 4:7

 Phil. 2:13

 1 Pet. 4:11

b. In Luke 11:5-8 what phrase do you think is the key to the man's persistence?

c. The man's awareness that he had nothing to set before his guest was the key to his effective waiting. If we think we can supply the need ourselves, we won't be able to continue in prayer until we receive God's supply.

Haven't you felt that at times? We have nothing to set before our children for family devotions unless God gives it to us. We have nothing to set before our neighbors, our Sunday School classes, all those who need to receive something from God. Satan wants to blind us to that fact and make us believe that through studying, or our natural abilities, we can give what is needed. Our attitude should be that of the psalmist in Ps. 60:11.

One of the signs hung by the decorating committee at our church dinner honoring graduates amused me: "I could not wait for success, so I went on without it." How foolish, I thought, to fail to take the time for the necessary details that success requires!

Then the truth hit me. Now I often quote a slightly modified form of this sign to myself as a warning: "I could not wait for the Holy Spirit, so I went on without Him." That thought always brings me up short. The assurance that the Holy Spirit brings may simply be a peace, a strong confidence, or a knowledge that God has heard.

4. How does Satan often blind us to our need of God's help?

◆ How We Know We're Waiting

A couple of simple tests determine if we're truly waiting on God. The psalmist said, "My soul, wait thou only upon God; for my expectation is from him" (Ps. 62:5, KJV). "It is comparatively easy," said E. M. Bounds, "to wait upon God; but to wait upon Him only is, I suspect, a difficult and rare attainment."[4] Yet those who wait are the ones God longs to find. He will give us our hearts' desires if we truly look to Him. Too often, though, we look to Him in prayer, but when we leave the place of prayer, we also leave our dependence upon Him to work. In His time He will work; He will do all we trust Him to do. But our waiting must continue beyond our prayer time.

1. Here are some guidelines to consider when we are waiting on God. If I am truly keeping my eyes on Him to meet my needs:

___ I don't get upset if my plans are changed.

___ I don't feel alarmed if my expectations are not met.

___ I'm at peace, although it appears God is not attending to my need.

___ I don't look to anyone but God to remedy the situation.

A friend had gone to many interviews looking for a job. One day, after months of looking, she was again turned down. "If God had given me a job with a salary paying many thousands," she commented, "we would have said, 'Isn't God good?' But God is just as good when He asks me to wait."

2. When we hang on to faith during disappointment, something within us deepens. Superficial piety gives way to spiritual growth. If God always answered our prayers quickly, we would be shortchanged. The benefits of waiting—of holding on to our confident expectation that God is faithful —are so profitable to us that God in His grace and mercy often delays answers to our prayers.

As we wait, our faith grows more daring. What are some of the benefits of waiting mentioned in the following verses?

 Ps. 27:14

 Isa. 40:31

 Ps. 37:34

A second test is our level of activity. This sounds like a paradox. On one hand we're doing nothing; on the other we're doing everything we can. Waiting does not mean inactivity; it means persevering. It means we exercise self-control to do whatever is necessary to express our strong desire.

The root word for *passive* and *passion* is the same, meaning *to endure.* While waiting, the heart is both passive and passionate, refusing to act on its own but passionate in looking to God.

To wait does not imply inactivity or lack of personal exertion; it means merely that our hope of aid and salvation is in God. We're not truly waiting on God unless we're doing all we can, but still we have our hope in God.

Paul wrote, "And the Lord direct your hearts into . . . the patient waiting for Christ" (2 Thess. 3:5, KJV). The Greek word for patient waiting is *huponome*. In ancient secular literature there is a story of a soldier who was decorated for his *huponome*, or his patient waiting. This soldier had not sat in his rocking chair patiently waiting for the battle to end—he had been on the front lines and had held steady in the thick of the action.

3. Often the most difficult period of waiting is the time beyond prayer—the time of patient waiting. I can wait in prayer, trusting God to help, but if I truly wait on Him beyond prayer:

___ I exercise self-control to accomplish my part.

___ I remember that God's work is by faith (1 Tim. 1:4), and I keep working even when it appears I'm accomplishing nothing.

___ I don't look at apparent results, because God's ways are not my ways.

God asks us to patiently wait—to wait on Him in prayer and then maintain a focused desire even beyond prayer. "Though it tarry, wait for it; because it will surely come" (Hab. 2:3, KJV). Though He tarries, wait for Him. The Holy Spirit will come.

God is never in a hurry, but neither is He ever late. An evangelist was coming to our home for Sunday dinner, and as I prayed for the Lord to make our visit a profitable one, I knew He had granted my request. Dinnertime was almost finished, though, and the conversation had just been usual chitchat. As I carried in the dessert, I cried with what John Wesley referred to as his "inner voice," "But, God, I know You heard me. Please help us." Somehow over dessert we began discussing answers to prayer. It was after four o'clock before we stirred from the table. I doubt any of us will forget that afternoon.

4. His "on time" answers are often referred to by us as "last minute" answers. Can you recall times when it seemed God answered at the last minute?

Scriptural Role Model

Why should I wait for the LORD any longer?" (2 Kings 6:33), the king of Israel asked in disgust. The Arameans had cut off the Israelites' food and water, and they were hungry.

Elisha had probably encouraged the king not to surrender but to wait for the Lord's deliverance. The king had had enough of waiting. What was his solution? Kill Elisha. Often, when we feel we can't wait any longer on the Lord, our solutions are destructive also.

Elisha promised God's deliverance in just one more day. The king's messenger scoffed at Elisha's assurance, so he was not permitted to eat of the abundance God provided.

Those words "Why should I wait for the Lord any longer?" often seem the most appropriate just before God's gracious answer. Read 2 Kings 6:24—7:20 for the entire story.

Memorize

"Wait for the LORD and keep his way. He will exalt you to inherit the land" (Ps. 37:34).

Prayer

Thank You, Lord, for teaching me that You delight in my waiting. Help me to delight in You enough to wait. Help me to wait until I mount up with wings as eagles, run without being weary, walk without fainting. I pray this in Jesus' name. Amen.

8

EXPECT AN ABUNDANCE

What a blessed prospect in my work—to know that even when the answer is long delayed, and there is a call for much patient, persevering prayer, the truth remains infallibly sure—"My God hears me."[1]

—Andrew Murray

Introduction

Often God grants larger blessings than we expect. Our intercessions count for more than we anticipate, more than we imagine. "When we came back from the mission field, I fully intended to get a job," a friend said. "But one Sunday morning the Lord impressed me with the words, 'You pray for Russia, and I'll supply your needs.'"

So instead of getting a job, she spent her time praying for Russia. Soon God began giving her beyond what she had even thought to ask. Free furniture arrived. Various people brought in *matching* pieces for their living room. Someone's discarded table that had been refinished was just right for my friend.

"One of the ways the Lord supplied my needs was to make me content," she said. "I'm happy with what we have."

We can ask for much; we can think of more. But God's capacity to give is, as stated in the Greek, "beyond everything." Sometimes when we pray, God says, "No, not yet"; at other times, "No, I love you too much"; but sometimes He says, "Yes, I thought you'd never ask," or even "Yes, and a whole lot more."

God's answers are always perfect. When we'd say God came "in the nick of time," God says, "When the time had fully come" (Gal. 4:4). If our prayer isn't answered even though we're trusting, God is waiting for the proper time.

Discussion and Questions

"I discovered the secret," said Aguiar Valvassoura, pastor of a large Church of the Nazarene in Campinas, Brazil. "It's not how big our faith is, but how big our God is. My faith is simple, but my God is extraordinary."

He continued, "God's telephone number is 333—that is Jer. 33:3: 'Call unto me, and I will answer thee, and shew thee great and mighty things, which thou knowest not'" (KJV). When his congregation increased from 200 to 600 and needed a larger building, he began to "ring up God." God replied, "Ask Me what you want Me to do for you." Rev. Valvassoura discovered that "A great God is waiting for great requests so He can give great responses." God supplied them with not only a larger church building but also an additional $250,000.

The word *mighty* in Jer. 33:3 means inaccessible. God says if we call upon Him He will give us the inaccessible! Let's look at what God calls an abundance and at one way to show God we want an abundance—united praying.

◆ God's Amazing Abundance

1. Has God ever given you exceedingly abundantly above all you could ask or think, as He promises in Eph. 3:20? "Now unto him that is able to do exceeding abundantly above all that we ask or think" (KJV)—this verse piles superlatives upon superlatives.

God "is able to [carry out His purpose and] do superabundantly, far over and above all that we [dare] ask or think—infinitely beyond our highest prayers, desires, thoughts, hopes or dreams" (Eph. 3:20, AMP.). Read this verse in different versions of the Bible and write down the phrases that encourage you.

2. God has repeatedly done more than His people have thought to ask or imagine. Let's consider some of the exceeding abundant answers God has given in the past.

a. If you had been one of the Israelites about to follow Joshua across Jordan River, would you have believed for dry ground to walk on? Read Josh. 3. What would have been the most you would have hoped for?

b. God delighted in not only giving His people passage through the river but also repeatedly giving them dry ground to walk on. See Exod. 14:16, 21-22, 29, and 2 Kings 2:8.

c. When God provides deliverance, it is so complete it is as though He says, "I'm going to give you such a deliverance that you won't have a trace of difficulty clinging to you." His grace provides abundantly more than we would think to ask. What difficulty are you experiencing now? God has plans for your total deliverance. Think on Isa. 55:8-9. Do you think our requests sometimes limit God?

d. When Jesus suggested that the apostles feed the 5,000, they knew He was asking the impossible. That would take eight months' wages! But Jesus was preparing to give beyond what they would dare to ask or think. Read Mark 6:30-44.

e. Notice that Jesus not only provided an all-you-can-eat fish dinner for 5,000 men, but He also provided a whole basket for each man who helped serve. God's super-abundance is seen best by those who are serving others for Him. Have you ever done something for the Lord and been surprised by how He repaid you for every effort or for the time you spent?

3. What do we do when someone is in great need and we'd love to provide an abundance of help? "All I can do is pray for him," I heard someone sigh recently as though there was small chance she could really help her friend. But Jesus did not say to Peter, "I'll strike Satan with a rod of iron," or "I'll provide you with a legion of angels to protect you." He simply said, "I have prayed for you" (Luke 22:32). Prayer was the *most* He could do. What does this say about Jesus' high view of the effectiveness of prayer? Does our view of prayer reflect His?

4. Paul wanted the Ephesians to understand how great their power in intercession was to be. How does he describe it in Eph. 1:18-20?

The Wesley Bible comments on these verses, "If our problem is no bigger than raising Christ from the dead, God can take care of it."

5. Jesus not only did more than those in the past asked or thought, but He also is doing the same today. God is answering your prayers in ways you are not even imagining. How do the following verses express God's desires to give abundantly beyond our imaginations?

 Isa. 65:24

 1 Cor. 2:9-10

God's delays are always filled with purpose, for He is not concerned with time—He is concerned with *timing*. Augustine fell deeper and deeper into sin, even though his mother, Monica, was faithfully praying for him. God may have been able to grant her much more in the end than if He had answered her when she first began her earnest praying.

6. Thinking of God is like thinking of space—however far our imaginations travel, infinitely more exists. Read Paul's prayer in the verses just before the promise in Eph. 3:20 (Eph. 3:14-19). What were some of his requests?

Especially notice the large request in the last phrase. Rather than allowing his requests to discourage him, they reminded Paul of God's great power.

7. In what specific areas of your life do you need to experience God's power now? Memorize Eph. 3:20-21. What do these verses say to you? What promise can you claim?

Satan whispers, "Your prayers are worthless. You might as well quit trying to believe." But then we read 1 Pet. 1:7, and the Spirit responds: "Your faith is precious to Me! One day your faith that is now being tried will result in praise, honor, and glory!"

God is doing far more through our praying than we can possibly know!

◆ An Abundance Through United Prayer

God multiples the results when we unite. When two or more people prevail together, their prayer power is not only added together but also multiplied. In medicine a drug reaction called "synergism" parallels this principle. Some medicines by themselves are ineffective against certain diseases, but when combined with another medicine, they accomplish much more than either could alone.

C. Peter Wagner tells that when he was young he attended "horse pulls." One of the strongest horses could pull 7,000 pounds and another an amazing 9,000 pounds. But when the two horses were hitched together, they could pull 33,000 pounds.[2]

We can be praying with others, though, and still pull only our individual loads of 7,000 or 9,000 pounds each if we are not praying for the same thing at the same time. When we all desire the same thing, with one leading in prayer and the others either silently or aloud saying a heartfelt, "Yes, Lord," our prayers become synergistic.

Many lightbulbs shining together make a bright light. But if they are concentrated into one light beam, they give a laser-beam effect capable of penetrating the hardest substance. Think of your agreeing in prayer as focusing your light into a laser beam that God can use to penetrate those "inaccessible" situations.

1. Satan fears the powerful results of united prayer, so he tries to make us feel foolish praying aloud with others. Here are some suggested ways to overcome the fear of praying in a group:

- Try praying aloud when you are by yourself.

- Ask the Holy Spirit to help you pray.

- Be willing to feel foolish if necessary.

- Think of prayer as a private conversation rather than as a performance.

Can you think of other ways to overcome this fear?

2. What do Lev. 26:8 and Matt. 18:19-20 suggest about the rewards of praying with others? Why do you think God encourages us to pray with others by His promising great returns?

3. The early Christians had group prayer meetings. What were some of the results? See Acts 2:1-2; 4:31; and 12:7.

One summer some of us met for prayer each Monday through Friday morning at church. On our prayer list was a neighborhood woman someone had contacted but who had refused to come to church. We prayed daily, "Dear Lord, save Patty, and her husband if she has one." That fall she still showed no interest in attending church but agreed to attend a home Bible study if we would find a babysitter. God had prepared her heart. During the first class she gave her heart to the Lord. Now she and her husband host weekly Bible studies in their home for their neighbors.

4. "Here is one alone, no one with him. . . . It is painful effort and unhappy business" (Eccles. 4:8, AMP.), wrote Solomon, lamenting the perils of aloneness. "Two are better than one; because they have a good reward for their labour" (v. 9, KJV). Also read verse 12, and apply it to our need to have united prayer.

5. We need to be close enough to others so that there can be prayer support. Why did those in Judg. 18:28 not have anyone to help them?

A praying group can make an impact. Our pastor told the man who arranged home prayer meetings, "When I walk into the pulpit on Sunday morning, I can tell if your group met to pray for the services this week."

6. Do you have at least one other person with whom you pray regularly? If not, consider how you could unite in prayer with others. Maybe your solution will be to do as one

mother and daughter who live in different states do—pray together weekly on the phone.

You are blessed if you find a partner with whom you can agree in prayer and claim the promise in Matt. 18:18-20.

Scriptural Role Model

God does for us much more than we could anticipate when we act in faith and obedience.

"Give me this mountain" (Josh. 14:12, KJV), insisted Caleb. Then because he boldly claimed the mountain, his children were blessed. "I will give him [Caleb] and his descendants the land he set his feet on, because he followed the LORD wholeheartedly" (Deut. 1:36).

We get a glimpse of God's fulfillment of this promise through an account of Caleb's daughter, Acsah. Caleb gave her to Othniel, who attacked and conquered Kiriath Sepher (see Josh. 14:15 and Judg. 1). One day she urged Othniel to ask her father for a field. When she asked, her father gave her the upper and lower springs. Where did she get the initiative to ask for the field?

Because her father had the aggressiveness to say, "Give me this mountain," his daughter also had what it took to say, "Please, may I have this field?" Her father's boldness made a difference in whom she married and in her ability to be aggressive. Our determined praying, "Give me this mountain," will have long-range effects on our families.

Caleb reminded Joshua that Moses had promised, "The land on which your feet have walked will be your inheritance and that of your children forever" (Josh. 14:9). *The land our feet touch* speaks of active participation. Once we've conquered land, it is for us and for our children. As the Holy Spirit leads you, you may wish to tell your children verses the Lord has given you for them. The land you've taken for them is theirs to claim also.

Memorize

"Now to him who is able to do immeasurably more than all we ask or imagine, according to his power that is at work within us, to him be glory in the church and in Christ Jesus throughout all generations, for ever and ever!" (Eph. 3:20).

Prayer

Dear Lord, You have made the heavens and the earth by Your great power. There is nothing too hard for You. You have promised that if I call, You will answer and show me great and mighty things. Teach me to ask for large requests so You can give large responses. I pray this in Jesus' strong name. Amen.

APPENDIX

SUGGESTIONS FOR LEADERS

Prayerfully Prepare

If you have a desire to lead a Bible study, consider that desire to be a gift from God. "Delight yourself in the LORD and he will give you the desires of your heart" (Ps. 37:4). God never gives you a desire to do a task for Him without providing all you need to accomplish it. Your most important qualification for this role is a sense of dependence on the Lord for His perfect provisions.

Lorne Sanny said, "Prayer is the battle; witnessing is taking the spoils." It's just as true to say, "Prayer is the battle; leading a small group is taking the spoils." You will lead with more confidence if you have prayed until you are trusting God to do His work in the group. Through prayer you gain a sensitivity to the Holy Spirit, so you can allow Him to guide the discussion according to the needs of the group.

As you study, seek to find from the Word a truth that excites you. Your excitement for the Word will be contagious. The psalmist wrote, "Blessed is the man . . . who finds great delight in his commands" (Ps. 112:1). *The Living Bible* adds that such a person "shall have influence and honor" (v. 9, TLB).

If the truths you share have reached only your intellect, they will likely reach only the intellect of those in your group also. But if the truths have reached your heart and changed your life, then there is a great chance they will reach your group members' hearts and be life-changing for them as well.

Rely upon the Lord to be the teacher, because spiritual truths must be taught by the Spirit. Isaiah 55:10 promises that the Word will be seed to the sower and bread to the eater. Your role is simply to sow the seed. As you do, God promises to provide the miracle of turning it into bread for those who receive it. Before every group meeting, ask God to provide spiritual bread for each one coming.

In the Tabernacle, there was always to be "the bread of the Presence" on the table "at all times" (Exod. 25:30). As you trust Him, God will always provide the exact bread each one needs that day. When you are tempted to think your supply of seed is exhausted, claim 2 Cor. 9:10: "Now he who supplies seed to the sower and bread for food will also supply and increase your store of seed and will enlarge the harvest of your righteousness."

Lead with Confidence

Be willing to share how God has worked in your life. Paul asked that his listeners follow him as he followed Christ. "Whatever you have learned or received or heard from me, or seen in me—put it into practice" (Phil. 4:9). As you allow the group members to see how you follow Christ, you not only show them how to follow Him, but you also provide the motivation. Many times Christians know what they must do to follow Christ but simply need the leadership of one who is wholeheartedly committed to obedience. Be that person for those in your group.

Keeping the Bible study alive and friendly is imperative. Your own attitude is a key factor in the group's enthusiasm. Develop a genuine interest in each person's remarks, and expect to learn from each individual. Concentrate on developing acceptance and compassion in the group.

Don't be afraid of silence following your asking a question. Give everyone time to think. Use "What do you think?" questions. These can help keep the discussion from seeming pressured or unnatural, since there is no such thing as a wrong answer to such a question.

Remember that your goal is not simply to lead an interesting discussion, but also to help group members understand and apply God's Word so it becomes life to them. "They are not just idle words for you—they are your life" (Deut. 32:47).

Occasionally suggest, "Next week let's bring to our group the verses that have especially ministered to us." Usually a verse becomes special when it meets a personal need, so group members will often share needs as well. Studying Scripture develops bonds of true friendship.

Remember Mal. 3:16 when enjoying the breaking of spiritual bread that occurs in group Bible studies: "Then those who feared the LORD talked with each other, and the LORD listened and heard. A scroll of remembrance was written in his presence concerning those who feared the LORD and honored his name." The Hebrew word for *listened* paints a picture of a mother bending over to listen to her children. Imagine God listening to you speak of Him and telling His recording angel to record your conversation in a journal in heaven!

"The lips of the righteous know what is fitting" (Prov. 10:32). Lead with confidence, because the Lord will help your words be appropriate as you learn to depend on Him.

Practical Tips

"In his heart a man plans his course, but the LORD determines his steps" (Prov. 16:9). As you make plans to respond to the desires He has given, the Lord will direct your steps and provide the specific guidance needed.

Although these lessons assume that those who are studying are Christians, welcome all who wish to join you. In the Early Church, the Lord added to their number. He is still Lord of the harvest and knows whom to draw. He will give a desire to all those who should be a part of your group. Depend upon the Lord to direct those who would profit from the study to attend. Edith Schaeffer stated that the workers at L'Abri Fellowship—a Swiss chalet opened by Francis and Edith Schaeffer for young people with philosophical questions—asked God to bring those who should come there to study and to keep away those who should not.[1] (It will be difficult for a majority to participate in the discussion if the group is larger than 10 or 12.)

Unless you are meeting as a Sunday School class or other regularly scheduled meeting at church, the ideal setting would be the home of a hospitable member of the church. Trust the Lord for details regarding time of meeting and place for weekly group meetings. Perhaps you could meet once when everyone can come, and then determine the details.

If you, as the leader, come early, you do more than set a good example. You also communicate your enthusiasm and delight in the group.

Begin on time, even if not all members are present. Be sure chairs are set up so latecomers can easily join you. Don't ignore latecomers, but don't let them disrupt the session. Greet them warmly, and then return to the study.

If you decide to include refreshments, a sheet can be available at the first meeting inviting those to sign who would like to provide refreshments.

Begin with prayer. Prayer is more than a transition from small talk to Bible study. You are providing the group with a consciousness that they are in God's presence.

Give time for prayer requests either before the opening or closing prayer. If someone has a special need, ask for volunteers who will spend 5 or 10 minutes during the next week in prayer for that person. Twelve 5-minute periods of prayer equal an hour of prayer! Send around a sheet of paper with the prayer request written down, and ask group members to write down how many minutes they will pray, to help them feel that they have indeed committed themselves to prayer.

You may want to begin each session by reviewing memorized scripture. Encourage group members to write down either the suggested verse or a passage that challenges or encourages them and reflect on it during the next week. They will find it beginning to affect their motives and actions. We forget quickly what we read once, but we remember what we ponder and act upon.

A few of the questions will be most easily understood if the *New International Version* is used.

Rather than moving mechanically through the written questions in each lesson, you may want to prepare some of your own questions. Write them out in advance and ask yourself if they are relevant and if the responses will teach what you think is important in this lesson. Avoid asking anything that is so personal the group members might find it threatening, unless you are willing to respond to the question first. As you share how God has convicted, encouraged, or instructed you through His Word, others will be drawn into sharing also.

End on time. If you say the study will be over at 9:00, end at 9:00. Then if any want to stay and visit, they can. This allows those with schedules to keep, or children to pick up, to exit without feeling they are missing part of the study.

Keeping in contact between weekly meetings is important. Make the burdens of your group members your own, and let them know you are praying for them. When they are absent, call to tell them you missed them, but don't pressure them to attend.

You are "God's workmanship, created in Christ Jesus to do good works, which God prepared in advance for us to do" (Eph. 2:10). All you need for this study has been pre-planned by Him.

Additional Chapter Comments
Chapter 1

People are seldom motivated to pray by being told they should spend 15 minutes (or longer) in prayer daily.

But once we catch a vision of God's desire to fellowship with us as He did with Adam and Eve in the Garden of Eden, then our natural response is one of wanting to come close to Him.

"God is most glorified in us when we are most satisfied in Him," writes John Piper in *The Pleasures of God*.[2] He states in the introduction of this book that what we need more than anything else is to know and love God—the great, glorious, sovereign, happy God of the Bible. "Very few people think of God as supremely happy. . . . The volcanic exuberance of God over the . . . welfare of his people is not well-known."

For your own heart preparation for this group meeting, meditate on Pss. 35:27 and 149:4.

Additional Notes:

Chapter 2

The last question in the section "The Power of Praise" deals with being able to praise God at all times. How could Paul say, "Give thanks in all circumstances, for this is God's will for you in Christ Jesus" (1 Thess. 5:18)? What enabled the psalmists who wrote of pain, suffering, and of being pursued by enemies, to inspire others to praise?

The psalmists' secret was that they looked at everything in the light of God's sovereign power and control and His unfailing love and mercy. Without such knowledge, the psalmists would have been defeated also. "I had fainted unless I had believed to see the goodness of the LORD" (Ps. 27:13, KJV). It was only as they chose to believe that an all-powerful God is good that they could with reverent praise write of cruelty, sickness, and even death.

For instance, Ps. 63 was written at the time of Absalom's rebellion. Yet despite David's grief, he wrote, "Because your love is better than life, my lips will glorify you" (v. 3). He was not being insensitive to his son, but he was trusting in the love of the One who controlled all things.

We do not chide those in the midst of grief or pain when they aren't praising the Lord, but we can pray that God will reveal His love to them in ways they can grasp.

Additional Notes:

Chapter 3

Andrew Murray taught, "Little of the Word with little prayer is death to the spiritual life. Much of the Word with little prayer gives a sickly life. Much prayer with little of the Word gives more life, but without steadfastness. A full measure of the Word and prayer each day gives a healthy and powerful life."[3]

The Word turned into prayer yields a healthy prayer life. George Mueller testified that often he could not pray as he desired until he focused his heart on a Scripture verse.[4] It's good to read the Scripture devotionally, looking for ways to let His Word express your day's concerns. When you find a promise that expresses the desire of your heart, God is pleased for You to hold it before Him until He answers.

Additional Notes:

Chapter 4

You cannot overemphasize the need to be dependent upon the Holy Spirit in prayer. Richard Trench wrote, "We must pray in the Spirit. . . . Do not address yourselves to prayer as to a work to be accomplished in your own natural strength. It is a work of God, of God the Holy Ghost, a work of His in you and by you."[5]

In prayer, as in all of our spiritual life, God declares it is "not by might nor by power, but by my Spirit" (Zech. 4:6). Without God's help we do not even have the ability to stir ourselves to pray. "There is no one who calls on Your name, who stirs himself up to take hold of You" (Isa. 64:7, NKJV).

Certainly we must depend upon the Spirit to help us teach this truth. Although we can try to coach someone in how to pray in the Spirit, we learn to do it as we follow the Spirit in prayer.

Additional Notes:

Chapter 5

Our depth of desire is critical to effective praying. What if we can't seem to pray with deep desire? First, ask the Holy Spirit to teach you how to long deeply for those needs you bring to Him. Perhaps in this as in many other situations, we have not because we ask not (see James 4:2).

Also, consider if your requests are in step with the Spirit. The Holy Spirit will not deepen our desires for selfish requests. Often when we sense the request the Spirit would enable us to pray, it is not the same request we would have made on our own. God knows how to answer our request much better than we know how to ask. Learning to listen and to follow the desires of the Holy Spirit adds great joy to our praying.

Additional Notes:

Chapter 6

Most of us realize the value of taking a list with us to the grocery store, and surely when approaching God we should at least be as prepared as we are when we go to the store. The more accessible we keep our prayer list, the more we can use it throughout the day.

Notice the command God made to Moses about Pharoah in Exod. 4:21: "See that thou do all those wonders before Pharoah, which I have put in thine hand" (KJV). God is still putting into our hands wonders He wants to do. Often these wonders are simply desires He gives us. He is saying, "Keep bringing these before Me. Ask, seek, knock, and these wonders will be opened. See that you lose none of what I want to give you."

Encourage those in the group to share any answers to prayer they've had after praying regularly for a need. They might also consider what it would mean to them to have someone praying daily for them. As their leader, you should be sure each one in your group is on your daily prayer list.

Additional Notes:

Chapter 7

In chapter 6 we studied the value of simply mentioning names to God in prayer. In this chapter we're learning to wait on God. Whether we regularly mention names to God or pray persevering prayers, we still wait on His timing and His response.

Jesus told the disciples to go into Jerusalem to wait for the promise of the Father. (See Acts 1:4.) We can almost imagine impetuous Peter saying, "So many are dying without hearing about Christ. Why should we wait?" But waiting is not a delay.

"Be filled with the Spirit," wrote Paul in Eph. 5:18, and the verse could as accurately be translated, "Keep being filled with the Spirit." The Amplified Version reads, "ever be filled and stimulated with the (Holy) Spirit." Again and again we need the refilling of the Spirit, and the Holy Spirit always responds anew to those who wait. You may want to discuss why God made waiting a prerequisite to receiving the Holy Spirit. Also, why is it equally imperative for us to make tarrying a priority today?

Additional Notes:

Chapter 8

There may be those in your group for whom prayer has been a disappointment. They say they can't believe God because they once tried prayer and "it didn't work." Perhaps the following illustration will help them.

Our prayer life can have three stages—childhood, adolescent, and adulthood. In childhood, Johnny believes everything. His mother says, "God will always be there for you," and he thinks, "Great—I'll always have what I want."

Then his mother gets sick and Johnny prays, "God, heal my mother," but his mother dies. At this point Johnny has a couple of options. He can enter a rebellious adolescent stage and think, "God didn't heal my mother, so prayer doesn't work." A second option would be for Johnny to say, "What did Mother mean when she said God would always be there for me? Maybe she meant God would be there for me in my suffering." Johnny will regain the joy of childhood by surrendering his ideas of how God should answer his prayers.

My friend said her father-in-law went to the hospital, and his wife asked her to pray that he wouldn't have to have surgery. "Frankly, I wasn't comfortable with her request. I prefer to pray for God's will in a situation rather than for what I think is best." Her adult response says to God, "I trust You to choose what is best, and I accept Your choice because I know You'll cause all things to work together for good for me because I love You."

Additional Notes:

Notes

Chapter 1
    1. A. W. Tozer, *The Knowledge of the Holy* (New York: Harper and Row Publishers, 1961), 107.
    2. William Barclay, *Hebrews Daily Study Bible* (Philadelphia: Westminster Press, 1957), 36.

Chapter 2
    1. Jack Taylor, *The Hallelujah Factor* (Nashville: Broadman Press, 1983), 173.
    2. Evelyn Christenson, *What Happens When God Answers Prayer* (Wheaton, Ill.: Victor Books, 1994), 184.
    3. Paul E. Billheimer, *Destined for the Throne* (Fort Washington, Pa.: Christian Literature Crusade, 1975), 120.
    4. Taylor, *The Hallelujah Factor*, 172.
    5. William Dryness, *Themes in Old Testament Theology* (Downers Grove, Ill.: InterVarsity Press, 1979), 165.
    6. Dick Eastman, *The Hour That Changes the World* (Grand Rapids: Baker Book House, 1984), 103.

Chapter 3
    1. W. Graham Scroggie, *How to Pray* (Grand Rapids: Kregel Publications, 1955), 14.
    2. Wesley Duewel, *Mighty Prevailing Prayer* (Grand Rapids: Francis Asbury Press of Zondervan Publishing House, 1990), 291.
    3. Sue Monk Kidd, *God's Joyful Surprise* (San Francisco: Harper and Row, 1987), 182-3.
    4. Dick Eastman, *The University of the Word* (Ventura, Calif.: Regal Books, 1983), 9.

Chapter 4
    1. Andrew Murray, *The Ministry of Intercession,* Marshall Pickering edition (Grand Rapids: Zondervan, 1988), 84.
    2. Duewel, *Mighty Prevailing Prayer*, 119.
    3. Christenson, *What Happens When God Answers Prayer*, 40.
    4. Hannah Whitall Smith, *The Christian's Secret of a Happy Life* (Westwood, N.J.: Fleming H. Revell, 1952), 165.
    5. Carole Mayhall, *Can a Busy Christian Develop Her Spiritual Life?* (Minneapolis: Bethany House Publishers, 1994), 55.

Chapter 5
    1. Quoted in David M'Intyre, *The Hidden Life of Prayer* (Minneapolis: Bethany House Publishers, 1993), 27.
    2. Duewel, *Mighty Prevailing Prayer*, 71.

Chapter 6
    1. Andrew Murray, *The Prayer Life* (Salem, Ohio: Schmul Publishers), 92.

2. Vonette Bright, *Prayer and Praise Diary* (San Bernardino, Calif.: Here's Life Publishers, 1981), 10.

3. Eastman, *The Hour That Changes the World*, 82.

4. Edith Schaeffer, *Common Sense* Christian Living (New York: Bantam Books, 1984), 226.

Chapter 7

1. E. M. Bounds, *The Praying Heart* (Bloomington, Minn.: Garborg's Heart 'n Home, 1989).

2. Sue Monk Kidd, *When the Heart Waits* (San Francisco: Harper and Row Publishers, 1990), 21-23.

3. Adam Clarke, *Clarke's Commentary* (New York: Abingdon Press, n.d.), 3:340.

4. E. M. Bounds, *The Praying Heart.*

Chapter 8

1. Andrew Murray, *The Ministry of Intercession*, 108.

2. C. Peter Wagner, *Churches That Pray*, Video Seminar Series (Ventura, Calif.: Gospel Light, 1994).

Appendix

1. Edith Schaeffer, *L'Abri* (Wheaton, Ill.: Tyndale House Publishers, 1976), 124.

2. John Piper, *The Pleasures of God* (Portland, Oreg.: Multnomah, 1991), 216.

3. Quoted in Duewel, *Mighty Prevailing Prayer*, 290.

4. Ibid., 292.

5. Ibid., 109.

For more information about Aletha Hinthorn or Women Alive Ministries, direct correspondence to:

Aletha Hinthorn
c/o Beacon Hill Press Marketing Department
P.O. Box 419527
Kansas City, MO 64141